LANDSCAPE & GARDEN PRODUCTS BUYER'S GUIDE

Over 2,700 Products
From 700 Suppliers

A Desktop Reference from
The Editors of Home Planners

HOME PLANNERS, LLC
Wholly owned by Hanley-Wood, Inc.
Tucson, Arizona

Published by Home Planners, LLC
Wholly owned by Hanley-Wood, Inc.

Editorial and Corporate Offices:
3275 West Ina Road, Suite 110
Tucson, Arizona 85741

Distribution Center:
29333 Lorie Lane
Wixom, Michigan
48393

Rickard D. Bailey/CEO and Publisher
Stephen Williams/Director of Sales & Marketing
Chuck Tripp/Director of Retail Sales
Cindy Coatsworth Lewis/Director of Publications
Jan Prideaux/Senior Editor
Paulette Mulvin/Project Editor
Sara Lisa Rappaport/Manufacturing Coordinator
Paul Fitzgerald/Senior Graphic Designer
Vicki Frank/Publications Coordinator
Brenda McClary/Publications Assistant

Project Manager: Kathleen M. Hart
Copywriter and Landscape and Garden
Consultant: Maureen Gilmer
    www.gardenforum.com™

Photo Credits
Front Cover: (clockwise from top right) photo courtesy of James Eaton; Classic Garden Ornaments, Ltd.®; John Deere Worldwide Commercial and Consumer Equipment Division; Netherlands Flower Bulb Information Center; Ames Lawn and Garden Tools.

Back Cover: Maureen Gilmer

Pages 1, 5, 9, 13, 16, 18, 20, 26, 29, 31, 34, 38, 43, 46, 48, 54, 57, 59, 65, 126: Maureen Gilmer
Page 36: Ursa Major Corporation

First Printing: March 1999

10 9 8 7 6 5 4 3 2 1

Printed in the United States of America

Library of Congress Catalog Card Number: 98-75684

ISBN: 1-881955-55-9

CONTENTS

How to Use The Buyer's Guide

Trying to find the best and most appropriate landscape and garden products can be a daunting effort. You can try gathering catalogs and advertising material and even visit Web sites (though there are hundreds) and sooner or later, you'll have a wealth of information and resources. But there's an easier and more comprehensive way.

Begin with the *Landscape and Garden Products Buyer's Guide*, the one-stop reference that includes the latest information for hundreds of manufacturer's, growers and suppliers. You'll find information about more than 700 companies and over 2,700 products, all in this handy reference tool!

The guide is a snap to use. Products are organized into nineteen main categories and further defined by more specific products within those categories. Looking for a source for daylilies? Turn to TREES, PLANTS AND GROUNDCOVERS and find the product heading *daylilies* for a list of sources. Then, to contact that source, turn to the Company Index starting on page 100 for complete address and telephone information about each of the suppliers. In some cases, there is also a FAX number and an E-mail or Internet address. We've also included a useful Product Index on page 126, with cross references to give you the most complete sourcebook for landscape and gardening products.

Some products are so unique or hard to find, we included it at the end of the grid pages as only a few growers or suppliers may offer it. Information for these companies may also be found in the Company Index.

Looking for additional reference material? Check the Book and Software Sellers Index on page 125 for sources for the latest in gardening and landscaping titles and computerware.

But, we don't just offer information. As a special bonus, we've included some of our favorite landscaping tips and a section of 15 landscape plans for which you can order installation instructions and plant lists regionalized for your specific area. These are just a few of the plans for landscapes offered by Home Planners for its readers. If you'd like to see more, call 1-800-322-6797 to order our plan books, brimming with landscape plans, deck plans and outdoor projects. We're here to help you make the most of your landscape and garden projects—which start with *Landscape and Garden Products Buyer's Guide*.

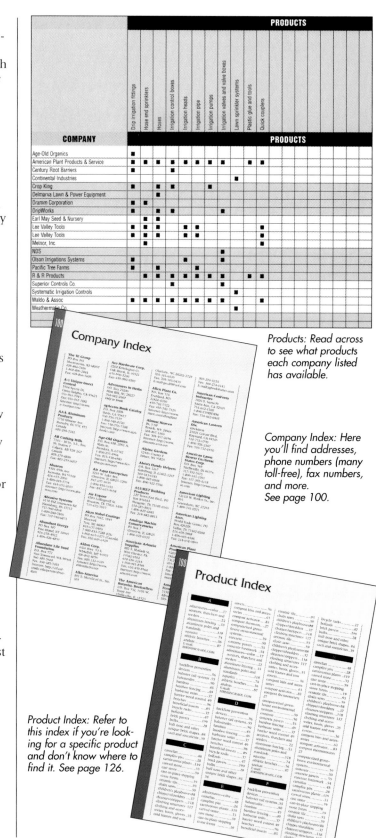

Products: Read across to see what products each company listed has available.

Company Index: Here you'll find addresses, phone numbers (many toll-free), fax numbers, and more. See page 100.

Product Index: Refer to this index if you're looking for a specific product and don't know where to find it. See page 126.

Concrete and Masonry

Concrete is a plastic material. This means that you can shape it like clay and it retains that shape indefinitely. A process known as "imprinting" uses metal stamps on freshly poured and colored concrete to turn an ordinary slab into faux stone or brick paving. But concrete is also sold in manufactured units. These units are either structural or pavers. Structural block units are used to build walls, and have special qualities that allow the use of steel reinforcement. Pavers may fit together like a puzzle or be simply square or brick shaped. They are not used to build, but are laid out on a prepared level base.

Manufacturers pour concrete into molds that produce both kinds of units, available in a variety of earth-tone colors. Concrete blocks have various finished surfaces such as adobe-look slump block and faux granite split-faced block. Interlocking pavers are popular because they fit together into complex patterns and are available in many different colors that allow a great deal of creativity in the finished product.

Brick is equally as popular but a bit more expensive. Brick is now sold in many different colors and finishes from imitation used brick to smooth iron stone. Brick can be laid on top of a concrete slab with mortar, or laid edge-to-edge on a prepared sand base without mortar.

Ceramic tiles are also used in paving, set over a poured concrete base. Tiles are not thick enough to lay on sand as with brick. Whenever you look at tiles for outdoor paving, be aware of slick finishes and glazes because they can be very slippery when wet. Ceramic tiles used outdoors must also be frost proof for your immediate climate. Tiles that are porous absorb water, then during a freeze, the water expands and severely damages the tile. For cold climates, some of the worst offenders are imported tiles from Mexico.

The prices for concrete and masonry units vary considerably depending on the kind you choose. One of the most overlooked expenses is the delivery charge because even the cheapest concrete block is very heavy, and it takes quite a bit of material to do just a small patio. Be sure you allow for such costs when you buy because a material that must be shipped across country will have far more overhead than one manufactured locally.

Whether you have a contractor build this part of your landscape, or if you do it yourself, above all research your material before you buy. Check unit price, longevity, frost resistance, and keep a sharp eye out for hidden shipping charges. Above all, explore the entire market before you choose because you'll be pleasantly surprised at how many new and creative products are now available in unit masonry.

Concrete and Masonry

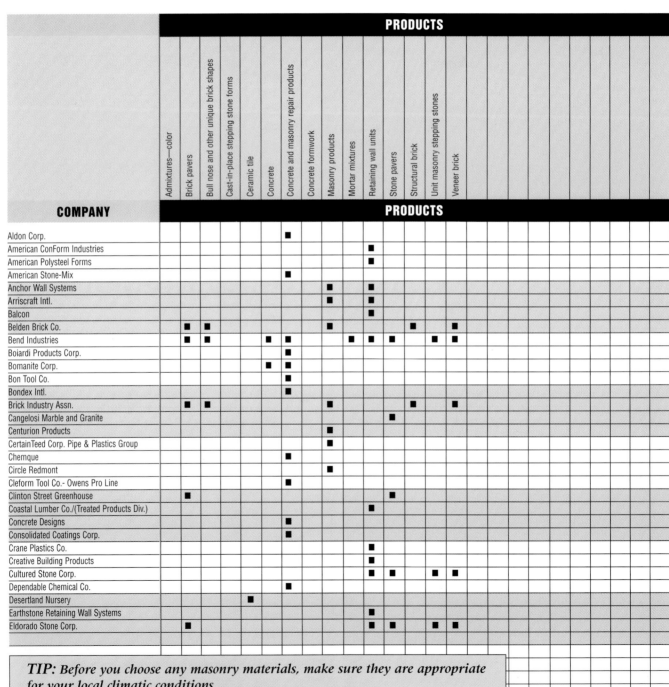

COMPANY	Admixtures—color	Brick pavers	Bull nose and other unique brick shapes	Cast-in-place stepping stone forms	Ceramic tile	Concrete	Concrete and masonry repair products	Concrete formwork	Masonry products	Mortar mixtures	Retaining wall units	Stone pavers	Structural brick	Unit masonry stepping stones	Veneer brick
Aldon Corp.							■								
American ConForm Industries											■				
American Polysteel Forms											■				
American Stone-Mix							■								
Anchor Wall Systems									■		■				
Arriscraft Intl.									■		■				
Balcon											■				
Belden Brick Co.		■	■						■			■			■
Bend Industries		■	■		■				■	■	■	■		■	■
Boiardi Products Corp.							■								
Bomanite Corp.						■	■								
Bon Tool Co.							■								
Bondex Intl.							■								
Brick Industry Assn.		■	■						■			■			■
Cangelosi Marble and Granite											■				
Centurion Products									■						
CertainTeed Corp. Pipe & Plastics Group									■						
Chemque							■								
Circle Redmont							■								
Cleform Tool Co.- Owens Pro Line							■								
Clinton Street Greenhouse		■									■				
Coastal Lumber Co./(Treated Products Div.)											■				
Concrete Designs							■								
Consolidated Coatings Corp.							■								
Crane Plastics Co.											■				
Creative Building Products											■				
Cultured Stone Corp.											■	■		■	■
Dependable Chemical Co.							■								
Desertland Nursery						■									
Earthstone Retaining Wall Systems											■				
Eldorado Stone Corp.		■									■	■		■	■

TIP: Before you choose any masonry materials, make sure they are appropriate for your local climatic conditions.

PRODUCTS

Company	Admixtures—color	Brick pavers	Bull nose and other unique brick shapes	Cast-in-place stepping stone forms	Ceramic tile	Concrete	Concrete and masonry repair products	Concrete formwork	Masonry products	Mortar mixtures	Retaining wall units	Stone pavers	Structural brick	Unit masonry stepping stones	Veneer brick
Fero Corp.							■		■						
Flexi-Wall Systems							■								
General Shale Brick									■						
Glen-Gery Corp.		■	■						■	■			■		■
Grani-Decor Tiles												■			
Haddonstone (USA)												■			
Hoglund Landscape Construction		■									■	■			
Increte Systems							■				■				
Isokern Fireplaces/Earthcore Industries									■		■				
Jamo									■						
Karnak Corp.							■								
Keystone Retaining Wall Systems											■				
Kraft Tool Co.									■						
Lee Valley Tools				■											
London Tile Co.		■													
Macco							■								
Macklanburg-Duncan							■								
Multi-Seal Pacific Corp.							■								
Muralo Co.							■								
National Concrete Masonry Assn.	■						■		■		■				
Old Carolina Brick Co.		■	■								■		■	■	■
Pacific Clay Brick Products									■						
Package Pavement Co.							■								
Pave Tech		■					■								
Paveloc Industries											■				
Petmal Supply Co.		■	■		■		■				■	■		■	
PL Adhesives & Sealants/ChemRex							■								
Plastival											■				
Quality Systems							■								
The Quikrete Cos.							■								
Redland Brick (Cushwa Plant)		■	■										■		■
The Reinforced Earth Co.											■				
Risi Stone Systems											■				
Rocktile Specialty Products												■			
Rockwood Retaining Walls											■				
SF Concrete Technology											■				
Simpson Strong-Tie Co.							■								
Slope Block											■				
Sonneborn/ChemRex							■								
Stone Construction Equipment						■				■					
Stone Forest												■			
Summitville Tiles		■	■											■	
Super-Tek Products							■								
Trenwyth Industries									■						
Trus Joist MacMillan								■			■				
Uni-Group USA											■				
United Gilsonite Laboratories							■								
Valley View Industries		■													

See Company Index for address and phone information.

COMPANY	Admixtures—color	Brick pavers	Bull nose and other unique brick shapes	Cast-in-place stepping stone forms	Ceramic tile	Concrete	Concrete and masonry repair products	Concrete formwork	Masonry products	Mortar mixtures	Retaining wall units	Stone pavers	Structural brick	Unit masonry stepping stones	Veneer brick
Versa-Lok Retaining Wall Systems											■				
Western Red Cedar Lumber Assn.											■				
Whitacre-Greer	■								■						
WR Bonsal Co.							■								
WR Meadows, Inc.							■								
Xypex Chemical Corp.							■								

See Company Index for address and phone information.

Decorative Concrete Wall Systems
American Technocrete Corp.
Superior Concrete Products

Imprinted Concrete
Bomanite Corp.

Veneer Stone
Cultured Stone Corp.
Rocktile Specialty Products

After dark, the garden is a very different place. Unfortunately the stars and moon aren't reliable sources of light to make a landscape usable at night. But when illuminated with carefully placed and adjustable outdoor lighting, it can become a festive or mysterious space.

The standard 110 volt outdoor lighting requires an electrician to install because the water and moisture of the garden makes electrocution a very real possibility. These systems must be encased in conduit with junction boxes, and it is all permanently installed at one time. These high-intensity lights are capable of illuminating the tops of tall palm trees or large buildings.

Security and safety lighting is of growing importance today and can be connected to motion sensors that turn them on as you or an intruder walks by. Fixtures can be mounted on the wall of your house or high up on poles where a much larger area may be illuminated. This high-voltage lighting is also suitable for outdoor sports because it can light a very large area completely with few shadows or dark corners.

It is important when using strong lighting to keep your neighbors in mind. Nobody wants bright light coming in their bedroom window at night, and if the next-door landscape is enjoying its own creative landscape lighting, it can be ruined by your over-bright flood lights.

Most people today are using 12 volt lighting in the landscape. Complete kits are sold at home improvement stores. A relatively new introduction, these systems require only a 110 volt outlet to operate all the lights. You can even buy a photo cell or a timer so they turn on and off automatically. Anyone can install them, too—all you need is a screw driver to attach the lights to a flexible wire fed by a transformer, plugged into an outdoor outlet. Step-up transformers are available if you need more lights than the standard transformer allows. The wire threads through the landscape and can sit on top of the ground or just below it. Most people cover the cords with decorative bark mulch.

Outdoor lighting comes with different types of fixtures designed for specific uses. Adjustable uplights illuminate things from below. Down lights or tree lights shine downward and are often attached to tree branches, shade arbors or along the top of a fence. "Mushroom" or path lights are used to highlight walking surfaces, making them safer and showing people where to go.

Electrical Materials

Adjustable uplights have bullet shaped housings attached to long plastic stakes. The heads can be moved up and down to light up a subject from the most ideal angle. The stakes can be moved at will to further control the effect. These positions may be moved as the plant changes with the seasons or grows larger. If you put an uplight in front of a subject it will be fully visible. If you uplight from behind, it is seen in silhouette.

Step or path lights are plastic shaped like a mushroom with a long, straight stem and a flying-saucer shaped head that casts light downwards all around it. Other styles are shaped like a question mark and are made of more expensive metals. Use these on walkways, steps, along stepping-stone routes, at hazardous crossings and around the driveway to keep visitors off the lawn edge.

The night landscape is a place for everyone to enjoy at an affordable price. Whether you're lighting a tennis court or a tiny Zen garden, there is a product designed especially for you, your budget and the nightscape of your dreams.

Electrical Materials

COMPANY	Aluminum poles and standards	Fiberglass poles and standards	Garden and leisure area lighting	Lamps	Low-voltage landscape lighting	Ornamental poles and standards	Security lighting	Sports and parking area lighting	Wood poles and standards
Alsto's Handy Helpers		■			■				
American Arborist Supplies		■						■	
American Lantern Div./Inteletron			■						
American Lighting			■						
American Lighting Assn.			■						
American Site Furniture			■						
Architectural Landscape Lighting			■						
Ardee Lighting			■						
Argee Corp.			■						
BB&S Treated Lumber			■						
Beacon Products			■						
Bend-A-Lite			■						
Berry Hill Limited	■					■			
Brandon Industries			■	■		■			
Brass Light Gallery			■						
Calger Lighting			■						
Canaren (Palwa By Canaren)			■						
Carlon Electrical Products			■						
Classic Lamp Posts			■						
Cotter's Tree Service		■							
Country Casual			■						
Desertland Nursery			■						
Dreamscape Lighting Mfg.			■		■				
Eagle Electric Mfg. Co.			■						
Eclipse Lighting			■						
FC Lighting			■						
Fiberstars			■						
Flos USA			■						
G & R Trellis & Supply Co.									■
GE Lighting			■						
GE Lighting Systems			■						
Genie House			■		■		■		
Guth Lighting			■						
Halo Lighting/(A Brand of Cooper Lighting)			■						
Hanover Lantern			■						
Herwig Lighting			■						

See Company Index for address and phone information.

TIP: To avoid the Las Vegas effect, don't use colored lenses on your outdoor lighting fixtures.

COMPANY	Aluminum poles and standards	Fiberglass poles and standards	Garden and leisure area lighting	Lamps	Low-voltage landscape lighting	Ornamental poles and standards	Security lighting	Sports and parking area lighting	Wood poles and standards
.hessamerica			■						
High-Lites			■						
Hinkley Lighting	■		■		■		■		
Hoglund Landscape Construction			■		■	■			
Holophane Corp.			■						
Hubbell Lighting			■						
Hunter Fan Co.			■						
Idaho Wood			■		■			■	
Intelectron			■						
International Energy Systems			■						
Justice Design Group			■						
Kichler Lighting			■						
Lee Valley Tools					■				
Lighting by Hammerworks			■						
Lightolier			■						
Lightway Industries			■						
Liteway			■						
Mel Northey Co.			■						
Mid-America Building Products Corp.			■						
Morlite Systems			■						
Nessen Lighting			■						
Newstamp Lighting Co.			■						
Old Strathcona Garden Shoppe			■		■				
Osram Sylvania			■						
Panasonic			■						
Philips Lighting Co.			■						
Point Electric			■						
Precision Multiple Controls			■						
Prescolite-Moldcast			■						
Progress Lighting			■						
Quality Lighting			■						
RAB Electric Mfg. Co.			■						
Raylux			■						
Regent Lighting Corp.			■						
Rejuvenation Lamp & Fixture Co.			■						
Roberts Step-Lite Systems			■						
Roy Electric Co.			■						
Sea Gull Lighting Products			■						
SNOC			■						
Solar Energy Industries Assn.			■						
Southern Intl.			■						
Starfire Lighting			■						
Sun Garden Specialities			■	■	■				
Sunstar Lighting			■						
Sure-Lites/(A Div. of Cooper Lighting)			■						
Swivelier			■						
Sylvan Designs			■						
Targetti USA			■						
Task Lighting Corp.			■						
Thomas Lighting/Consumer Div.			■						
TIR Systems			■						
Tivoli Industries			■						
Tollmark Corp.			■						

See Company Index for address and phone information.

COMPANY	Aluminum poles and standards	Fiberglass poles and standards	Garden and leisure area lighting	Lamps	Low-voltage landscape lighting	Ornamental poles and standards	Security lighting	Sports and parking area lighting	Wood poles and standards													
Trimblehouse Corp.		■																				
UNITEC		■																				
U.S. Gaslight		■																				
WAC Lighting Co.		■																				

See Company Index for address and phone information.

Computerized Greenhouse Environmental Systems
Shelter King (A Div. of Crop King)

Grow Lights
Growers Supply

Nearly every landscape has a fence of one kind or another. It may be a simple backyard board fence or an elaborate New Orleans style cast-iron showpiece. Fences are there to serve a purpose, and in the process we try to make them look beautiful as well.

Fences in landscapes are used as enclosures. They provide security from the public as well as visual privacy. The ability to separate your yard from the world outside is entirely contingent on your fence. Heights range from the lowly picket to extra tall barriers, all controlled by local building codes. In general, rear yard fences are rarely allowed to exceed six feet in height, and front yard fences, if allowed at all, are limited to about three feet high.

Wood fences were the most common kind of fencing in the past, but with skyrocketing lumber prices—particularly redwood—new metal and plastic fencing assemblies are growing in popularity. However, there remain specialty wood-work companies that are creating pickets, arbors and gates for the high-end vintage markets.

Plastics were slow to come on the market because of weaknesses to ultra-violet light. Newer formulas have extended their life span considerably, so that now you can buy a white plastic board, rail or picket fence with confidence. Most are offered in white, and the two most popular styles are the three-rail ranch fence and little picket fences. These fences never peel or need repainting because the color is through-out rather than just on the surface.

Metal fencing is expensive and this kind of material is more likely used for gates and gateways than fences. Metal gates do not sag and make very secure portals. Best of all their transparent qualities preserve the sense of openness.

Deer fencing is a new but essential product in today's market. Originally the tall prison-camp style was all that was available, but new strategies have

Fences And Gates

reduced cost and visibility. Nearly transparent plastic netting systems are effective and safe. Electric netting is also available now that keeps rodents and other small pests out of gardens as well.

Fencing is essential for safety, security, beauty and the viability of plants and gardens. Review the new products and discover the new choices that are not only more affordable, but long lasting, too. When you discover the costs involved, you'll agree that it's best to build it once and build it right.

Fences And Gates

COMPANY	Aluminum fencing	Bamboo fencing	Plastic fencing	Vinyl fencing	Wood fences	Wood gates	Wrought iron decorative fencing
AB Cushing Mills					▪		
Almost Heaven					▪		
American Technocrete Corp.			▪		▪		
Bow House/Bowbends					▪	▪	
Brock Deck Systems/Royal Crown Ltd.			▪				
Bufftech			▪				
The Burruss Co.					▪		
Burton Woodworks/A Div. of MHJ Group						▪	
Butler Box & Stake		▪			▪		
California Redwood Assn.					▪	▪	
Carlon Electrical Products				▪			
Cedarbrook Sauna					▪		
CertainTeed Corp. Pipe & Plastics Group			▪				
Coastal Lumber Co./(Treated Products Div.)					▪		
Country Casual					▪	▪	
Creative Building Products			▪				
Cross Vinylattice			▪				
Curt Bean Lumber Co.					▪		
Dalen Products			▪				
DEC-K-ING	▪						
DuraVinyl				▪			
Easy Gardener			▪				
Ensurco Duradek (U.S.)	▪						
Federal Wood Products					▪		
Feeney Wire Rope & Rigging	▪						
G & R Trellis & Supply Co.		▪					
Genova Products			▪				
Great Southern Wood Preserving					▪		
Heritage Vinyl Products				▪	▪		
Hoglund Landscape Construction					▪		
Kodiak					▪		
Kroy Building Products			▪	▪			
L.B. Plastics			▪				
Lee Valley Tools							▪
Mellco					▪		
Moultrie Mfg.	▪						

TIP: *Garden gates should be at least four feet wide to allow mowers and other equipment to go in and out without a struggle.*

See Company Index for address and phone information.

PRODUCTS

COMPANY	Aluminum fencing	Bamboo fencing	Plastic fencing	Vinyl fencing	Wood fences	Wood gates	Wrought iron decorative fencing
Park Place						■	
Philstone Fasteners					■		
P.L. Rohrer & Bro.				■			
Plastival			■				
Pompeian Studios						■	
Prudential Building Materials			■				
ReSource Building Products			■				
Royal Crown Limited/Triple Crown® Fence				■			
Southeast Wood			■		■		
Southern Pine Council					■		
Southern Sales & Marketing Group					■		
Sovebec					■		
Stanco Inc.				■			
Steel & Wire Products Co.			■		■		
Thermal Industries			■				
TR Miller Mill Co.					■		
Triple Crown Fence/Royal Crown Ltd.			■				
Universal Forest Products					■		
VinylGard				■			
Wavecrest Nursery	■						■
Western Red Cedar Lumber Assn.					■		
Western Wood Products Assn.					■		
Wood Innovations of Suffolk	■				■	■	

See Company Index for address and phone information.

Baluster Rail Systems
Style-Mark
Worthington Group

Balustrades
Haddonstone (USA)

Deer Fencing
Benner's Gardens

Ornamental Fencing
Leslie-Locke

Post Hole Drills
Hoffco

PVC Railing
Kroy Building Products
L.B. Plastics
Moultrie Mfg.
Stanco Inc.

Wood Polymer Fencing
Trex Co.

Woven Fences
American Willow Growers
  Network
Bamboo & Rattan Works

Fountains

There is nothing more refreshing and soothing after a long hot day than the sound of falling water. It appeals to something deep inside us that is very primal, and linked to the most fundamental need of life—water. If you were to compare two identical gardens, one with falling water and one with still water, the one with falling water is more appealing, hands down. It is the sound of water that is so attractive, and it is true that birds are irresistibly drawn to the glint of water drops in the garden—a sure wildlife magnet.

Not long ago only the wealthy could afford a water feature in their garden, but not any more! Micro technology, futuristic plastics and an explosion in suppliers makes the sound and beauty of falling water possible for even the most modest budgets. Each year the prices go down and the variety of styles expands considerably so that you no longer have just cherubs to choose from.

The greatest breakthroughs were the development of flexible plastic lining materials which are thick and resilient. They can be ordered

from a tiny backyard size to huge farm pond liners. Flexible liners allow you to dig a pond any shape or size you wish. Remember, however, that liners are vulnerable to exposure to ultraviolet sunlight which breaks down the plastic over time. When you work with this product be sure to use cantilevered coping stones to cover and protect the edges of the liner for increased longevity.

The other way to create an in-ground water garden is using prefabricated rigid fiberglass pond shells. Simply dig a hole, insert the shell, level it and fill in the soil around the edges. You may choose from a dozen sizes and styles which dictate the exact shape of your pond. These are stronger and more resistant to sharp objects than the flexible liner.

Once these in-ground pools are installed, you have the ability to arrange stones into a natural waterfall. You'll need a 110 volt outlet to power a submersible pump that will circulate the water. Then you may decide whether to create a living water garden with plants and fish, or keep it simple with chlorinated water.

The second group of water garden products are self-contained portable units as small desk-top fountains for balconies and decks, and even indoors! They are great wherever there isn't room for big freestanding units. You would be surprised at how much these tiny water works can transform the character of an atrium, or sunny porch.

Freestanding units are larger and push a great deal of water. They are quite heavy and require someone strong to move and place them in their final destination. These are the best at attracting wildlife and many are shaped like birdbaths on pedestals. Such a unit requires an outdoor outlet if it is not located next to a structure. It's not safe to run extension cords through the garden.

Wall fountains are a tradition in Italian gardens. They are made out of cast iron or bronze, and sometimes ceramics. A wall fountain is composed of a back plate with a design featuring a lion's head or other motif that serves as the spout. At the bottom of the back plate is a half basin that catches the water. All the plumbing and piping is either underwater or on the back. Just hang it up and plug in. These are very simple to install on wood fences, lattice panels or other surfaces where you can thread the cord out the back so it isn't visible. But if you have a stucco or masonry wall, use leafy plants or train a vine to cover up the cord.

Today you can spend $50 or $5,000 on a ready-made fountain. It can be created out of natural stone, concrete, ceramics, bronze, iron and even plastics. The finishes you choose can make cast concrete look like bronze, so don't settle for the tired old white. Look around—you'll be amazed at what you find.

Fountains

COMPANY	Electrical components	Filters	Fountain lighting	Fountain pumps	Fountains	Jet heads	Pipe and pipe fittings	Pools (shells and liners)	Water garden accessories
Age-Old Organics				■					
Air Aqua Enterprises			■	■		■	■		■
Berry Hill Limited					■				
California Acrylic Industries/Cal Spas					■				
Desertland Nursery					■				
DripWorks								■	
Earl May Seed & Nursery				■				■	■
Firestone Building Prod. Co.									■
Haddonstone (USA)								■	■
Hamlet & Garneau									■
Hoglund Landscape Construction	■	■	■	■		■	■	■	■
L & L Nursery Supply		■	■	■				■	■
Lee Valley Tools		■		■		■		■	■
Lily of the Valley Herb Farm									■
Northern Greenhouse Sales								■	
Old Strathcona Garden Shoppe				■					
Paradise Water Gardens		■	■	■		■		■	■
Patio Garden Ponds									■
P.L. Rohrer & Bro.		■	■	■		■		■	■
Pompeian Studios									
Resource Conservation Technology		■	■	■		■	■	■	■
Robert Compton, Ltd.					■				
Slocum Water Gardens		■	■	■		■	■		■
Stone Forest					■				
Stonewear, Inc.					■				
Straubel Stone Lightweight				■					

TIP: *A water garden must receive at least four hours of direct sunlight a day for water lilies to grow and bloom.*

See Company Index for address and phone information.

Fountains

COMPANY	Electrical components	Filters	Fountain lighting	Fountain pumps	Fountains	Jet heads	Pipe and pipe fittings	Pools (shells and liners)	Water garden accessories
Van Ness Water Gardens		■	■	■		■		■	■
Waterfall Creations	■	■	■	■	■	■	■	■	■
Wavecrest Nursery	■	■	■	■	■			■	■
Wicklein's Water Gardens		■	■	■				■	■
Wind and Weather					■				
Windy Oaks Aquatics		■	■	■		■		■	

See Company Index for address and phone information.

Chemicals and Aeration Supplies
Air Aqua Enterprises

Irrigation Systems

All plants require water—it's just that some need more than others. That's why today's watering systems are more diverse, and therefore more complicated to shop for than in the past. It helps, though, to know some of the terminology in order to be a savvy shopper by mail or at the home improvement store.

A traditional sprinkler system is called "spray irrigation." The pipes are permanent and underground. They are fed by a series of valves that may be manually activated, or turned on automatically by a time clock. This clock is the "brain" of the system and sometimes called the controller. Today's controllers are digital and give you practically unlimited ability to water as often as you want, when you want and for as long as you want just by pressing a few buttons.

The big variety is in sprinkler heads. Pop-up heads do just that—they pop up and spray when you turn on the system, then drop back and disappear when the water is off. This has always been a feature of lawn heads because you have to mow over the top of them. Today's space-age plastics have made it affordable to have pop-up heads everywhere, not just on the lawn. They make the sprinklers disappear into the landscape and are far more attractive than the old-fashioned flower bed heads that sit permanently on a fixed riser

for everyone to see.

Since the water crunch started out West and is now afflicting not-so-Western communities, new and more efficient technology has produced drip irrigation. This is a low-pressure system composed of black flexible tubing that is more often than not set out on top of the ground. It is designed to dribble water at each plant at a rate of one or two gallons per hour rather than the spray head rate of one to two gallons per minute. You can get electronic timers and other accessories for drip systems, too.

Micro-spray systems are half drip and half spray. That means that they are low pressure and use the same kind of tubing as a drip system, but the water is sprayed out of pencil-sized spray heads. They sit on the end of flexible tubing and are anchored by a little stake so you can move them around at any time.

The world of irrigation is growing rapidly. Ever since the advent of plastic saw-and-glue pipe back in the 1960s, systems have changed considerably. Above all they are easier for you to install and repair, so replacement parts are available at most home improvement retailers. But though it is simpler to do, the decisions are more plentiful as you sift through the options and find out what's best for you.

Irrigation Systems

COMPANY	Drip irrigation fittings	Hose end sprinklers	Hoses	Irrigation control boxes	Irrigation heads	Irrigation pipe	Irrigation pumps	Irrigation valves and valve boxes	Lawn sprinkler systems	Plastic glue and tools	Quick couplers
Age-Old Organics	■										
American Plant Products & Service	■	■	■	■	■	■	■	■		■	■
Century Root Barriers	■			■							
Continental Industries									■		
Crop King	■		■	■			■	■			
Delmarva Lawn & Power Equipment			■								
Dramm Corporation	■	■									
DripWorks	■		■	■				■			
Earl May Seed & Nursery		■	■								
International Irrigation Systems	■										
Lee Valley Tools	■	■	■			■	■				■
Melnor, Inc.		■									■
NDS								■			
Olson Irrigations Systems	■				■			■			
Pacific Tree Farms	■		■				■				
R & R Products		■	■	■	■	■	■	■		■	■
Superior Controls Co.				■				■			
Systematic Irrigation Controls									■		
Waldo & Assoc	■	■	■	■	■	■	■	■			■
Weathermatic Co.									■		

TIP: *Always install a filter on your drip or micro-spray system to catch particles in the water that could plug up the tiny emitter orifices.*

See Company Index for address and phone information.

Foggers
Ann Mann's Orchids
Olson Irrigations Systems

Hydroponic Supplies
Crop King
Nature's Control

Landscape Maintenance

Care of the landscape requires an array of equipment from things as small as a hand trowel to others as big as a garden tractor. Landscape care products varying considerably in both price and quality. The golden rule when it comes to buying hand tools is to plan on using it for a good part of your lifetime. This means that it won't be the cheapest one you find—more often than not the quality is expressed by high prices.

Hand tools with blades, such as hoes or pointed shovels, must be made of good strong steel. That way you can resharpen them with a hand file to make the work easier. The tool should have a strong hardwood handle that is free of cracks or splinters. There should be no rattle or movement when you shake it.Lawn mowers come in a huge array of sizes and types. Most are rotary types with a single spinning blade, but in areas where Bermuda and other warm-season grasses are the norm, reel mowers are still used. Clearly, rotary mowers are easier to maintain and sharpen which makes them a good buy. In fact, new models are called "mulching mowers" because they grind up the clippings super-fine and return them to the lawn as healthy organic matter.

Riding mowers can be pricey, but are great labor savers, particularly if you're not very strong. Riding mowers do have some limitations, and if you're a heavy person you need to buy a powerful one. They can also tip over on slopes so beware if your topography is challenging.

String trimmers have a thousand-and-one uses. They handle a variety of jobs such as trimming lawn grass around trees and other hard to reach spots, and are the best means to cut weeds down in areas too rough or inaccessible for mowers.

Hand pushed fertilizer spreaders are helpful for planting, fertilizing, and applying pest and disease control chemicals. They are excellent for top-dressing an organic lawn with manures and compost. Spreaders are designed in many sizes to suit every lawn from a postage stamp to city park.

Pruning Tools and Equipment

The gardener's most important tool is a strong pair of hand clippers. Clippers should fit comfortably in your hand so choose small ones if your hands aren't big or strong. Long handled clippers or "loppers" are equally important for cutting limbs too thick for hand clippers.

For limbs too thick for loppers use a manual pruning saw. The kind that folds up like a giant pocket knife is most convenient for gardeners. When you have a lot of heavy pruning, or if you must take down a tree, the chainsaw is your only alternative. Electric chainsaws don't offer nearly the power of gas driven models, and your freedom of movement is more limited by the cord.

Telescoping pole pruners allow you to reach high into trees to prune out unwanted growth. Light aluminum models are best. Choose one with a pruning saw attachment. The priciest models have little electric chainsaws at the end that make the annual pruning of fruit trees a snap.

Manual and power-driven hedge clippers are needed if you have sheared hedges in the landscape. Most people are using electric or gas driven models because they are so fast and really do a great job. For small yards or when hedges are near the house, use the electric models. Gas types are more trouble but are the only solution for very large properties.

Landscape Maintenance

PRODUCTS

COMPANY	Accessories	Aerators, thatchers and seeders	Chain saws	Chipper/shredders	Clothing and accessories, boots, gloves	Garden carts	Garden tractors and accessories	Hand tools	Herbicides	Lawn sprinkler systems	Leaf blowers	Mowers	Organic gardening products	Pest controls	Pesticides	Plant tags	Plant ties, twine, guy wires and connectors	Pots, flats and non-decorative containers	Power hedge clippers	Pruning tools	Rototillers	Sprayers	String trimmers and edgers	Tree trunk protectors	Wildlife products: bird baths, houses, feeders
A-1 Unique Insect Control													■												
Age-Old Organics													■												
Air Aqua Enterprises								■															■		■
Alsto's Handy Helpers								■											■	■		■	■	■	
American Arborist Supplies			■	■	■			■	■		■									■		■		■	
American Lawn Mower Co./Great States Corp.												■													
American Plant Products & Service	■				■			■	■						■	■	■	■		■		■		■	
American Standard Co./Florian Ratchet-Cut	■							■												■					
Amerigrow Recycling													■												
Arbor Systems LLC																					■				
Ardisam				■																	■				
Barreto Manufacturing																					■				
BB&S Treated Lumber																								■	
Bear Cat/Crary Co.				■																					
Bear Creek Nursery								■					■	■						■					
Benner's Gardens														■											■
Berry Hill Limited								■												■		■			■
Bio-Gard Agronomics													■												
BioLogic														■											
Bird-X																									
Bluebird International		■		■		■																			
Bonide Products													■	■	■									■	
Bosmere	■							■									■	■	■	■					
Bronwood Worm Farms													■												
Broyhill																						■			
Burlington Scientific Corp.													■	■	■										
Cape Cod Worm Farm													■												
Cart Warehouse						■																			
Carts Vermont						■																			
Century Root Barriers				■																				■	
Cepco Tool								■																	
Chimney King														■											
Classen Manufacturing	■	■																			■				
Clinton Street Greenhouse	■												■												
Colorblends by Schipper & Co.				■																				■	
Combustion Service						■																			

See Company Index for address and phone information.

PRODUCTS

COMPANY	Accessories	Aerators, thatchers and seeders	Chain saws	Chipper/shredders	Clothing and accessories, boots, gloves	Garden carts	Garden tractors and accessories	Hand tools	Herbicides	Lawn sprinkler systems	Leaf blowers	Mowers	Organic gardening products	Pest controls	Pesticides	Plant tags	Plant ties, twine, guy wires and connectors	Pots, flats and non-decorative containers	Power hedge clippers	Pruning tools	Rototillers	Sprayers	String trimmers and edgers	Tree trunk protectors	Wildlife products: bird baths, houses, feeders
Continental Industries										■															
Cotter's Tree Service	■		■	■	■			■			■									■			■		
Country Home Products													■							■	■		■		
Crop King													■	■	■	■						■			
Crosman Seed Corp.									■						■										
Dalen Products	■																								
David Bacon Fine Handcrafted Furniture																									■
Davidson Wilson Greenhouses					■			■	■				■		■	■		■		■			■	■	
Dawes Engine Generator			■	■			■				■	■							■	■	■	■	■		
Deep Root																				■				■	
Delmarva Lawn & Power Equipment	■		■	■	■		■	■			■	■								■		■	■		
Digger's Product Development Co.	■													■											
Direct Edge				■						■												■	■		
Dixon Industries												■													
Dorothy Biddle Service					■			■								■	■			■					
Dramm Corporation													■												
D.V. Burrell Seed Growers Co.		■						■														■			
Earl May Seed & Nursery								■	■				■			■	■	■		■		■		■	■
Easy Gardener																							■	■	
Emi Meade, Importer					■																				
Excel Industries												■													
Farm Wholesale Greenhouses													■				■							■	
Feeney Wire Rope & Rigging																	■								
Fehrman Industries						■	■																■		
Fiskars Lawn & Garden Div								■												■					
Florian Ratchet-Cut Pruning Tools					■			■												■					
Florida Mycology Research Center													■												
Florikan Southeast									■						■			■							
G & R Trellis & Supply Co.								■								■	■			■					
Garden of Delights													■												
Grasshopper Co.	■																								
Grimo Nut Nursery								■																	
Growers Supply						■													■						
The Guano Co. Intl.													■												
Heckendorn Equipment												■													
Heinze Plant Labels																■									
Heirloom Seeds													■			■									
Hickock Pruning Tools								■												■					
Hoffco																					■		■		
Hoglund Landscape Construction									■																
Hy Grade Planting Mix													■												
Hydro Turf		■																				■			
Ingersoll Equipment Co.				■			■					■									■				
IntAgra Deer-away														■											
Integrated Fertiltiy Management													■		■										
International Irrigation Systems																								■	
J.L. Matthews Co.			■		■			■												■			■		
John Deere/Consumer Equip. Div.	■	■	■				■					■						■		■	■	■	■		
Johnson Nursery	■												■			■	■			■					
Kadco USA						■																			■
Karl Kuemmerling, Inc.	■		■	■	■			■									■		■	■		■	■	■	
Kinsman Co.					■			■								■	■	■		■		■	■		■
Kramer Equipment								■												■					

See Company Index for address and phone information.

PRODUCTS

Company	Accessories	Aerators, thatchers and seeders	Chain saws	Chipper/shredders	Clothing and accessories, boots, gloves	Garden carts	Garden tractors and accessories	Hand tools	Herbicides	Lawn sprinkler systems	Leaf blowers	Mowers	Organic gardening products	Pest controls	Pesticides	Plant tags	Plant ties, twine, guy wires and connectors	Pots, flats and non-decorative containers	Power hedge clippers	Pruning tools	Rototillers	Sprayers	String trimmers and edgers	Tree trunk protectors	Wildlife products: bird baths, houses, feeders
Kunz Engineering												■													
L & L Nursery Supply									■				■		■	■	■	■		■					■
Lee Valley Tools	■		■		■			■				■				■	■			■					■
Liberty Seed Co.					■			■					■	■	■									■	
Little Wonder								■			■										■	■	■		
Little's Good Gloves					■																				
Living Stones Nursery																		■							
MacKissic				■							■										■	■			
Magic Circle Corp.												■													
Mainline of North America				■								■									■				
Mainline Tillers	■			■			■				■	■							■				■		
Mantis											■										■	■			
The Marugg Co.								■																	
Mary's Plant Farm								■									■			■					■
McCulloch Corp.	■		■								■												■		
MN Productions				■																					
MTD Pro								■														■	■		
Mushroom People													■												
Nature's Control													■												
Necessary Organics										■			■		■										
Nedia Enterprises													■						■						
Newtown Power Equipment			■	■			■													■	■	■	■		
Nitron Industries													■		■										
Nixalite of America														■											
Northeastern Associates		■		■												■				■	■		■	■	
Northwind Nursery and Orchards								■					■								■			■	
Norway Co.						■																			
Ohio Earth Food													■												
Old Strathcona Garden Shoppe								■					■			■	■				■				■
The Original Bug Shirt Co.					■																				
Pacific Tree Farms								■					■					■			■				
Parker Sweeper				■			■				■														
The Patriot Co.				■							■														
Pave Tech								■																	
Paw Paw Everlast Label Co.	■															■	■								
Perky-Pet Products																									■
Pinetree Garden Seeds	■				■	■		■	■				■		■	■	■			■		■			■
P.L. Rohrer & Bro.								■	■				■	■	■			■		■		■		■	■
Planet Natural													■												
Poston Equipment Sales		■		■							■	■									■	■			
Pratt's Power Equipment	■		■	■			■	■				■								■	■	■	■	■	
Pro Lawn Equipment												■													
Quinstar Corp.												■													
R & R Products	■				■																				
Reinco		■																							
R.J. Winmore	■							■																	
Rota-Trim Sales																							■		
Scag Power Equipment																							■		
Schlabach's Nuresey															■		■			■				■	
Schweiss Co.												■										■			
Sea Born/Lane													■												
Select Seeds - Antique Flowers													■												
Shredit Rotary Mower Blades												■													

See Company Index for address and phone information.

COMPANY	Accessories	Aerators, thatchers and seeders	Chain saws	Chipper/shredders	Clothing and accessories, boots, gloves	Garden carts	Garden tractors and accessories	Hand tools	Herbicides	Lawn sprinkler systems	Leaf blowers	Mowers	Organic gardening products	Pest controls	Pesticides	Plant tags	Plant ties, twine, guy wires and connectors	Pots, flats and non-decorative containers	Power hedge clippers	Pruning tools	Rototillers	Sprayers	String trimmers and edgers	Tree trunk protectors	Wildlife products: bird baths, houses, feeders
Simplicity Mfg.				■			■														■				
Southern Barks													■												
Southland Mower												■													
Steiner Turf Equipment				■			■				■	■													
Streator Unlimited					■	■																			
Sweepster		■																							
Systematic Irrigation Controls										■															
Textron Turf Corp.												■													
Tree Pro																								■	
Treessentials Co.																								■	
Tru-Cut												■													
Upper Hand Marketing								■																	
Valley View Industries	■																								
Van Bourgondien Bros.																■									
Vandermolen Corp.				■							■			■					■				■		
Waldo & Assoc								■							■	■			■					■	
Walker Mfg. Co.												■													
Wavecrest Nursery	■							■	■				■	■	■	■				■				■	■
Weathermatic Co.										■															
Wellington Leisure Products																	■								
Winged Weeder								■																	
Womanswork					■																				
Yeoman & Co.								■																	

TIP: All hedges are sheared slightly wider at the bottom so that the sides receive sun to keep the bottom branches from dying out for lack of light.

See Company Index for address and phone information.

Barrier Weed Control
Hoglund Landscape
  Construction

Beneficial Insects
A-1 Unique Insect Control
Nature's Control
Planet Natural

Fungicide
Necessary Organics

Grafting & Budding Supplies
Bear Creek Nursery
Northwind Nursery and
  Orchards

Post Hole Drills
Little Beaver Inc.

Protection Fabrics
Crop King
De Witt Co.
Reemay
Shelter King (A Div. of
  Crop King)

Protective Planting Bags
Bulb Savers

Pruning Sealer
IntAgra Deer-away

Spreaders
Wikco Industries

Trenchless Leaching
Flo-Well Water Management

Turf and Plants Heating/Cooling Systems
BioTherm Hydronic, Inc.

Vine Clip Fasteners
G & R Trellis & Supply Co.

Lawns And Grasses

Most homes in America have a lawn, and we spend huge amounts of time mowing and fertilizing to make sure it always looks its best. Today's lawns are planted with more disease-resistant, less water-consuming grass strains, although the old stand-bys are still out there.

Traditional lawns are planted from seed, and the variety should be well suited to your local climate and conditions. Seed is sold as a pure strain, mix or blend. A mix is composed of three or more grasses that are compatible. This makes the lawn more adapted to a variety of exposures. Seed blends are a combination of different varieties of the same grass. For example, a tall fescue blend may contain 'Bonsai,' 'Pixie' and 'Crewcut,' all named varieties that are bred for small stature and slow growth.

Some types of lawn seed are sold as "endophyte enhanced," which means that they contain a special fungus which will live inside the adult grass plant. It does not hurt the plant at all, but bugs find it absolutely distasteful. This futuristic biological technique is just the first of many new enhancements of turf grass to reduce pesticide use.

Turf grass lawns are also planted vegetatively from sod, sprigs or plugs. The sod industry is enormous and you can now buy practically any kind of lawn grass in sod rolls. Simply figure out how big your new lawn will be and then order the sod through a local garden center. It will be delivered to your door at the right time for your project. A you would with carpet, you simply lay out each roll on prepared lawn soil into a giant patchwork quilt. It takes about two weeks for sod roots to begin penetrating the soil.

Another vegetative way to plant is with plugs and sprigs. Plugs are like little pieces of sod which contain root, plant and soil. Sprigs do not have soil but are partially rooted. Either way they are planted one at a time into the lawn area at a certain spacing, and will eventually fill in the gaps to produce a beautiful green lawn. This method requires much more mulching, weeding and care than sod, but is less expensive and may be the only way to go with grasses not commercially grown at sod farms.

Among the new trends in the lawn industry is an attention to native grasses and meadow lawns that require much less water and chemicals. Native grasses are those that grow wild in America, and are often a part of prairie ecosystems. Blue gamma and buffalo grass have proved best adapted to lawns and are now widely grown commercially for planting by seed or plugs.

Meadow lawns are an alternative to the traditional mowed turf. These native grasses are allowed to grow tall and are combined with colorful wildflowers as they are in wild places. Colorful butterflies are attracted to the flowers, as are other beneficial insects which make the surrounding garden less vulnerable to harmful pests.

Today's lawns enjoy more varieties than ever before, advances in turf grass technology and a return to Mother Nature's lawn grasses. Whether you suffer from drought, bugs or rampant diseases, there may be resistant grasses and new equipment that can take the backache out of your backyard.

Lawns And Grasses

COMPANY	Mulch	Natural lawns	Seeds—grass	Sod	Sprigs
American Plant Products & Service	■				
Amerigrow Recycling	■				
Bark Plus	■		■		
Chas. C. Hart Seed Co.			■		
Clargreen Gardens	■		■	■	
Clinton Street Greenhouse	■	■	■		
Colorblends by Schipper & Co.			■		
Comstock Seed			■		
The Conservancy			■		
Crosman Seed Corp.			■		
Davidson Wilson Greenhouses			■		
DeGiorgi Seed Co.			■		
D.V. Burrell Seed Growers Co.			■		
Earl May Seed & Nursery	■		■		
Earthly Goods			■		
Feder's Prairie Seed Co.		■			
Florida Mycology Research Center			■		
Frosty Holly Ecological Restoration			■		
Hoglund Landscape Construction	■				
IntAgra Deer-away			■		
Integrated Fertiltiy Management	■		■		
Johnson Nursery			■		
L & L Nursery Supply	■		■		
Larner Seeds			■		
Lister's Sod Farm				■	
Native Gardens			■		
Northplan/Mountain Seed			■		
Ohio Earth Food		■			
Old Strathcona Garden Shoppe			■		
Pacific Tree Farms	■				
P.L. Rohrer & Bro.	■	■	■		
Plants of the Wild			■		
Prairie Ridge Nursery/CRM Ecosystems, Inc.		■	■		
Pratt's Power Equipment			■		
The Reveg Edge		■	■	■	
S & S Seeds			■		

See Company Index for address and phone information.

Lawns And Grasses

COMPANY	Mulch	Natural lawns	Seeds—grass	Sod	Sprigs
Seeds Trust: High Altitude Gardens		■	■		
Shooting Star Nursery			■		
Shredit Rotary Mower Blades	■	■			
Soils Plus Recycling	■				
Southern Barks	■				
Sovebec	■				
Stock Seed Farms		■	■		
Todd Valley Farms		■		■	
Vesey's Seeds	■		■		
Wavecrest Nursery			■		
William Dam Seeds			■		

See Company Index for address and phone information.

Bamboo
Burt Associates Bamboo
Pacific Tree Farms

Lawn Patch
Ampro Industries

Native Prairie Grasses
Carmel Valley Seed Co.
Feder's Prairie Seed Co.
Holland Wildflower Farm
Native Gardens
The Reveg Edge

Ornamental Grasses
Busse Gardens
DeGiorgi Seed Co.
Limerock Ornamental
 Grasses
Todd Valley Farms

R ailings are important parts of the constructed landscape. They protect the user from falling off decks and elevated surfaces and ensure children and pets are safely enclosed. Square rails come in all sizes and may be finish coated with rust and weather-resistant paints.

Handrails are crucial to steps, and in some communities they are strictly required by building codes. They should be conveniently sized to be used by the weakest senior citizen. They may be of wood with metal brackets to make sure they aren't cold in winter.

Cast or wrought iron are the two most decorative forms of ironwork. They are the most recognizable architectural detail in old New Orleans—used on balconies, railings and supports. Cast iron is made by pouring liquid metal into forms. This allows more ornamentation, but suffers a greater problem with rust, and poor-quality cast iron can be notoriously brittle. Wrought iron is more easily worked by heating and bending rods

Metal Fabrication

into creative patterns. It is stronger, less expensive and preferred for security barriers.

All fabricated metal must be properly primed and painted if it is to last. Rusting is the greatest challenge, not only because of the corrosion of the metal, but because rust will stain adjacent surfaces. Repainting at regular intervals is required, but compared to wood, all ironwork seems immortal.

Metal Fabrication

COMPANY	Decorative metalwork	Hand rails and railings	Ornamental metal handrails and railings	Wrought iron decorative fencing																		
									PRODUCTS													
Builders Edge	■																					
C & H Roofing/Country Cottage Roof	■																					
Ceilings & Interior Systems Construc. Assn.	■																					
Chimney King	■																					
DEC-K-ING		■																				
Decor Grates	■																					
Feeney Wire Rope & Rigging		■	■																			
Formglas	■																					
Heritage Finishes	■																					
Lee Valley Tools				■																		
Ludwig Industries	■																					
Macklanburg-Duncan	■																					
Moultrie Mfg.		■	■																			
The October Co.	■																					
Pompeian Studios				■																		
S. Parker Hardware Mfg. Corp.	■																					
Schluter Systems	■																					
Spiral Stairs of America		■																				
Steptoe & Wife Antiques	■																					
Strom Plumbing By Sign Of The Crab	■																					
Villagecraft Industries	■																					
Wavecrest Nursery			■	■																		

See Company Index for address and phone information.

Galvanized Steel Garden Accessories
Jomoco Products Co.

Metal Edging
Sure-Loc Edging Corp.

Metal Trellises and Arbors
Mary's Plant Farm

Topiary Frames
Topiaries Unlimited

Weather Vanes
Windleaves

There is a wide variety of products used today to color and seal various types of building materials such as wood and masonry. Wood of any kind expands when it gets wet because water is absorbed. As it dries the wood contracts leaving cracks behind. To extend the life of all outdoor woodwork, it should be sealed to reduce, and, hopefully, eliminate the repeated swelling and shrinkage.

Wood sealers are manufactured either clear, or containing a pigment. Clear sealers do nothing to change the appearance of the wood, although it will have a richer color right after application. Over time this "wet look" gets worn down. This is the best kind of product for retaining the natural beauty of high-quality redwood and cedar construction.

When dealing with Douglas fir and other woods, weathering can cause irregular discoloration. Using pigmented wood preservative will give it a better overall hue, but beware of those labeled "redwood" as this tends to be a very unnatural brick red. It's always better to choose a pigment that matches your house exterior or any other large structure in the landscape.

Wood stains and sealers are great cover-ups, too, because they won't peal like paint does. One problem that often afflicts fences is bleached arcs caused by sprinklers. A heavy body stain can cover that up, unify the fence, and give old boards new life.

A variety of new masonry sealers are designed to prolong the beauty of outdoor stone or brick work. Efflorescence is a term given to the white mineral buildup on masonry surfaces. As water passes through a wall it picks up lime and other minerals from concrete and mortar, transporting them to the outside face. The water evaporates but the white stuff remains. Even if you acid wash the masonry to get the efflorescence off, it will return unless you seal

Paint

the wall. Many of these sealers are clear and can be applied to all sides and the top of planter walls and even onto flat paved surfaces.

It's important to apply these products only during dry weather. In fact, it's good to have a few weeks of dry warm weather in order to have as little moisture trapped inside the wood or masonry as possible when its sealed. You can apply the products with brush, roller or spray machine. The key is to choose the right product for the material, apply according to instructions, and re-apply at recommended intervals.

Paint

COMPANY	Cleaners/strippers	Transparent finishes	Transparent stains	Transparent waterproofing sealers
The 3E Group		■		■
Abatron	■			
Abrasive Systems	■			■
Ace Hardware Corp.		■		
Akzo Nobel Coatings		■	■	
Aldon Corp.		■		■
Alko-America				■
Basic Coatings		■	■	
Benjamin Moore & Co.			■	
BiWood Flooring		■		
Bomanite Corp.			■	
BonaKemi USA		■	■	
Bruce Hardwood Floors		■	■	
Cabot/(Samuel Cabot Inc.)	■	■	■	■
Cuprinol	■		■	■
Daly's Wood Finishing Products	■	■	■	■
Dampney Co.		■		
DAP	■	■	■	■
Dean & Barry	■	■	■	■
Diedrich Technologies	■			■
Duckback Products/Superdeck Brand Products	■	■	■	■
Dura Seal Div. of Minwax Co.	■	■	■	
Dur-A-Flex		■		
Dutch Boy Professional Paints		■		
Dyco Paints		■	■	■
Fine Paints of Europe		■	■	
The Flecto Co.			■	
The Flood Co.	■	■	■	
Geocel Corp.				■
Gibson-Homans Co.				■
H & C Concrete Stain		■	■	
Harris Specialty Chemicals		■		■
ICI Paint Stores	■	■	■	■
KCI Coatings		■	■	■
Klean-Strip	■			■
Martin-Senour		■	■	

See Company Index for address and phone information.

> **TIP:** *Always seal the inside of a raised masonry planter to keep the moisture from passing through leaving a white mineral residue on the outside.*

COMPANY	Cleaners/strippers	Transparent finishes	Transparent stains	Transparent waterproofing sealers
Masters Choice		■		■
McGrevor Coatings	■	■	■	■
Minwax Co.	■	■	■	
Miracle Sealants & Abrasives	■	■		
Multi-Seal Pacific Corp.	■	■		■
Muralo Co.		■	■	
National Paint and Coatings Assn.		■	■	■
Northern Paint Canada	■	■	■	■
Old Masters	■	■	■	■
Olympic Paints and Stains		■		
Oregon Research & Development Corp.		■		■
Osmose Wood Preserving	■	■	■	■
Palmer Industries		■		■
Parex		■		
Parks Corp.	■	■	■	
Penofin-Performance Coatings		■	■	
Poly-Wall Intl.		■		
PPG Industries	■	■	■	■
Pratt & Lambert		■	■	■
Premier Wood Floors		■	■	
ProSoCo.	■	■	■	
Quality Systems	■	■	■	■
Samax Enterprises	■			
Sansher Corp.	■			
Sheffield Bronze Paint Corp.	■			
The Sherwin-Williams Co.	■	■	■	■
Standard Tar Products Co.		■	■	■
STO Finish Systems		■		
Super-Tek Products		■	■	
Surebond		■		■
Tarheel Wood Treating Co.			■	■
United Gilsonite Laboratories	■	■	■	
Wagoner Floor Safety Systems	■	■		
Wall Firma		■		
Weatherall Co.			■	■
William Zinsser & Co.	■	■	■	
Wolman Wood Care Products	■	■	■	■
Woodcraft Supply		■	■	
Wood-Kote Products	■	■	■	
WR Meadows, Inc.	■			
Xypex Chemical Corp.		■		
Yenkin Majestic	■	■	■	■
Zynolyte Paints		■	■	

See Company Index for address and phone information.

Deck Waterproofing—PVC
DEC-K-ING
DecTec

Greenhouse Shading Paint
American Plant Products &
Service

Paving And Surfacing

Paving is to the landscape what floor coverings are to the inside of your house. Paving sets the character of the interior and landscape.

Paving can be composed of units which are installed with masonry applications. But the most common paving is installed in a single application or "pour" where it hardens up into a single mass. These poured products require forming, which is the most labor-intensive part of the job.

Paving is used for patios, pool areas, walkways, driveways and sports courts. Patios are the most visible because they usually connect to the house, and at big glass sliding doors the paving ends up adjacent to interior flooring. The rule of thumb is to try and use a paving that is visually compatible so the indoor-outdoor transition is visually uninterrupted. This is why paving on patios is of higher quality than on other parts of a landscape.

Walkways are smaller and can range from broad front entry promenades to little side-yard walks that run down narrow gaps between buildings. Sidewalks average around three feet wide. Remember that a concrete mow strip poured around a lawn becomes a walkway if it's just slightly wider than the standard eight inches.

Driveways can be expensive because of their size, and are paved with either concrete or black asphalt. Blacktop is much less expensive than concrete and may be occasionally renewed by a slurry coat. Its chief weakness is moisture both while being installed and when it accumulates underneath a driveway. That's the source of "bird baths," the common term for the depressions that occur in old or very thinly laid asphalt driveways. Sports courts are treated much the same way as driveways but need not be quite as strong.

Turf stones were originally designed to create fire lanes in apartment complexes without sacrificing beautiful grass areas. These concrete waffle-shaped units lie just below the surface of the soil. They have open squares of soil that alternate with concrete, strong enough to support an emergency vehicle. Today they are used for front yard guest parking that is beautiful when unused but essential when entertaining.

Other alternative pavings are less solid but still widely used in home landscaping. Decomposed granite is among the most natural materials for pathways when rolled and packed in place. Gravels are sold by the size of each piece, with pea gravel a popular choice for pathways, sideyards and dog runs. One-inch gravel can be "crushed" with sharp edges that dig into the ground for driveway applications, and is very uniform in color. It can also be "river run"—rounded, multicolored, more natural and easier on the feet.

Decorative gravels are popular in Japanese Zen gardens, where dry steam beds and gravel fields are symbolic water courses. They are also common in very low-maintenance landscapes where there is a limited water supply. Gravel can be white, black and a brick red volcanic rock along with other specialty choices.

Paving is important to the usability and beauty of your landscape. Do not overlook delivery charges on gravel, and the costs of installation of turf block, because these charges can be surprising.

Paving And Surfacing

COMPANY	Brick pavers	Ceramic tile	Concrete	Concrete pavers	Gravels	Stone pavers	Unit masonry stepping stones
Belden Brick Co.	■						
Bend Industries	■		■	■		■	■
Bomanite Corp.			■				
Brick Industry Assn.	■						
Cangelosi Marble and Granite						■	
Clinton Street Greenhouse	■				■	■	
Cultured Stone Corp.						■	■
Desertland Nursery		■					
Eldorado Stone Corp.	■					■	■
Glen-Gery Corp.	■						
Grani-Decor Tiles						■	
Haddonstone (USA)						■	
Hoglund Landscape Construction	■			■		■	
London Tile Co.	■						
Old Carolina Brick Co.	■						■
Pave Tech	■						
Petmal Supply Co.	■	■				■	
Redland Brick (Cushwa Plant)	■						
Rocktile Specialty Products						■	
Stone Construction Equipment				■			
Stone Forest						■	
Summitville Tiles	■						
Valley View Industries	■						
Whitacre-Greer	■						

TIP: To be on the safe side and avoid a law suit, never use a paving with gaps big enough to catch the high heel of a woman's shoe.

See Company Index for address and phone information.

Grass Pavers
NDS
RK Mfg. Grassye Pavers

Surface Drain
Flo-Well Water Management

Playfield Equipment

Whether it is a jungle gym for the kids, or a volleyball court for teens, playfield equipment is big business. Prefabricated units take the guess work out of creating recreational amenities in residential backyards. You are assured the dimensions and materials have met national safety standards.

Wood has become popular because it blends in more naturally with the landscape. It is also softer and some believe it reduces the risk of injuries. The down side is that wood decomposes after awhile and longevity may be limited unless the units are built out of expensive foundation-grade redwood or pressure-treated wood. Some people have a problem with splinters, so it's important to make sure whatever you buy is adequately finished.

Space-age plastics have really changed the industry because they are affordable, lightweight and easy to install. It is essential to buy only those products indicated as UV stabilized plastics. This is because sunlight causes some plastics to become brittle, and over a short time cheaper products will begin to crack.

Metals are the most traditional material for swing sets, sports nets, basketball backboards and a dozen other popular products. Steel is heavy and is, by far, the strongest, most long-lived material on the market. However, it will eventually begin to rust if not painted or treated and can be difficult to transport due to weight. Aluminum is lighter and doesn't rust, but can be very expensive.

Metals should be painted or galvanized to reduce rusting, particularly if you live near the ocean. Corrosion is a serious concern there and often concrete posts and other less vulnerable materials are being used instead of metals in such difficult climates.

It's important to think about surfacing when you purchase any permanent play structures. Sand is no longer favored because it attracts neighborhood cats and produces a much harder surface than you think. Schools are now substituting sand with ground bark which is proving to be more resilient and a lot easier to transport. It's cleaner, too.

Play equipment provides hours of family fun, but remember that the kids won't be young forever. When choosing a place for a fort or climbing structure, plan to have a secondary use for that area later on. Turn it into a water feature or flower garden, even a vegetable plot if the exposure is right. Above all enjoy it now, knowing that your family need never leave home to have fun.

Playfield Equipment

COMPANY	Athletic benches	Climbing structures	Fitness trails	PRODUCTS																
Belson Outdoors	■																			
Kadco USA		■																		
Landscape Structures		■																		
RK Mfg. Grassye Pavers			■																	
Wavecrest Nursery		■																		

TIP: When the playground is in your own back-yard, you always know where the kids are.

See Company Index for address and phone information.

Outdoor Rubber Flooring
Petmal Supply Co.

Children's Playhouses
Handy Home Products

Pre-Engineered Structures

It's becoming downright expensive to hire a carpenter these days to build a shed or gazebo or a greenhouse. But fear not, because there are so many alternative structures to choose from that are already pre-engineered. That means that you can buy them partly or fully assembled, and have them delivered right to your home.

The latest craze in garden trellage is trump l'oeil, the art of illusion. Flat lattice panels are prefabricated to give the illusion of depth by creative use of perspective. Attach to an uninteresting flat wall and discover how much space you can gain without giving up an inch.

So many gardeners imagine a romantic gazebo as the central focus

for a landscape or flower garden. But hexagonal structures are not only difficult to design, they can be mind boggling to build yourself. Fortunately these are now sold in kits which are shipped in pieces and assembled on site. The kit takes all the guesswork out of the project and you get specialty finish work such as turned spindles and gingerbread. Gazebos can also be fitted with screens to keep the bugs out, and both ceiling fans and lights to make evening dining much more comfortable.

Another popular structure is the garden shed. Sold as kits or already completed structures, they come to you on a flat bed semi and are off loaded with a fork lift that puts it anywhere you want. The best part is that you need no foundation—place on pier blocks, concrete blocks or on an existing slab. They are offered in a variety of basic sizes and styles with windows or doors wide enough to accommodate your riding lawn mower.

Greenhouses are very important to a serious gardener. If well lighted they will extend an otherwise short growing season to nearly tropical day lengths. Some are built with wood frames, others with an aluminum or heavy-duty plastic structure. Instead of glass they now use translucent plastics which are safer and naturally diffuse sunlight. Styles range from Quonset to A-frames and the traditional peaked roof. You may want to consider an exhaust fan if you live in a very warm climate or a heater for very cold nights.

For less ambitious gardeners a cold frame is just a smaller box version of the greenhouse with a glass top. Position toward the south for maximum exposure in spring, and if you add an electric heater you can start your plants months ahead of time in spring and then pick up again in autumn for greens until Christmas. Cold frames have been an indispensable tool of home gardeners since pioneer days.

You might also want to try row covers which are simple plastic tent ribs, like Quonset huts covered with plastic sheeting that are set up over your vegetable garden plants. They protect against the biting cold and wind of fall, giving plants more time to ripen and prolonging the seasonal green harvest. You can also cover these ribs with shade cloth to protect your sensitive seedlings until they harden off. In fact, shade cloth in summer can be used to enhance the shading potential of any arbor and shelter over patio or potting area from midsummer sun.

Before you buy it's wise to get a good idea of how long these kinds of products will last in your climate. In the low lands of the deep South, termites and moisture may not make wood structures a good buy. Plastics suffer in the deep cold of the upper Midwest or the searing dry heat of the Desert Southwest.

Pre-Engineered Structures

COMPANY	Cold frames and row covers	Gazebos	Greenhouses	Membrane structures (tent-like)	Pergolas, arboretums and conservatories	Prefabricated shelters	Prefabricated wood trellage and arbors	Shade cloth	Sunrooms												
AAA Aluminum Products									■												
Abundant Energy			■		■				■												
Almost Heaven		■																			
ALUMET Building Products									■												
Amdega Machin Conservatories		■	■		■				■												
American Plant Products & Service	■		■					■													
Americana Bldg. Products By Hindman Mfg.									■												
Anderson Design/Garden Arches							■														
Artistic Enclosures									■												
BC Greenhouse Builders			■						■												
Berry Hill Limited			■																		
Bow House/Bowbends		■				■	■														
Brady Rooms									■												
Bufftech		■					■														
Burton Woodworks/(A Div. of MHJ Group)							■														
Caldera Spas & Baths		■																			
California Acrylic Industries/Cal Spas		■					■	■													
California Redwood Assn.		■	■				■														
Carolina Solar Structures			■		■				■												
Case Window & Door					■				■												
Circle Redmont			■						■												
Classic Post & Beam									■												
Classy Glass Structures		■	■		■				■												
Columbia Mfg. Co.					■				■												
Commonwealth Solar Rooms			■		■				■												
Contemporary Structures									■												
Craft-Bilt Mfg. Co.									■												
Creative Structures			■		■				■												
Crop King	■		■	■		■		■													
Cross Vinylattice							■														
Cumberland Woodcraft		■																			
CYRO			■		■				■												
Dalton Pavillions		■				■	■														
Davidson Wilson Greenhouses								■													
De Witt Co.								■													
Duo-Gard Industries			■		■				■												

See Company Index for address and phone information.

Pre-Engineered Structures

COMPANY	Cold frames and row covers	Gazebos	Greenhouses	Membrane structures (tent-like)	Pergolas, arboretums and conservatories	Prefabricated shelters	Prefabricated wood trellage and arbors	Shade cloth	Sunrooms
Dura-Bilt Products									■
D.V. Burrell Seed Growers Co.	■		■						
Earl May Seed & Nursery							■		
Easy Gardener								■	
Evergreen Systems Sunrooms					■				■
Farm Wholesale Greenhouses	■		■					■	
Florian Greenhouse			■		■				■
Four Seasons Solar Products			■		■				■
G & R Trellis & Supply Co.							■		
Garden Essence							■		
Gothic Arch Greenhouses			■						
Haddonstone (USA)		■							
Handy Home Products		■	■						
Hartford Conservatories									■
Heirloom Seeds							■		
Heritage Vinyl Products							■		
The Hess Mfg. Co.			■						■
Hoglund Landscape Construction		■					■		
Holland Log Homes Mfg. Co.									■
Houses & Barns by John Libby/Barn Masters					■				
JA Nearing Co.			■		■				■
JKR Design/Build		■	■						
Joyce Mfg.					■				■
Kroy Building Products		■	■						
Lee Valley Tools	■	■	■			■			
Legacy Timber Frames									■
Lindal Cedar Homes/Sunrooms									■
Living Stones Nursery						■			
Mason Corp.									■
Mellco							■		
Moultrie Mfg.		■							
National Spa and Pool Institute					■				
Northern Greenhouse Sales	■		■						
Omega Sunspaces			■						■
P.L. Rohrer & Bro.							■		
Plastics Research Corp.							■		
Plastival		■							
Rahn Trellis Co./(A Div. of MHJ Group)							■		
Rainbow Roof Systems by Madden Mfg.					■				
Reynolds Metals Co.			■						
Royalston Oak Timber Frames					■				■
Santa Barbara Greenhouses			■						
Scatton Bros. Awning Mfg.									■
Shelter King A (Div. of Crop King)	■		■	■		■		■	
SkyQuest			■		■				■
Skytech Systems			■		■				■
Southern Pine Council		■							
Southern Sales & Marketing Group			■						
Sun Room Co.			■		■				■
Sun Room Designs			■						■
Sunbilt Solar Products by Sussman			■		■				■
Sundance Supply			■		■				
Sunesta Products		■							

See Company Index for address and phone information.

COMPANY	Cold frames and row covers	Gazebos	Greenhouses	Membrane structures (tent-like)	Pergolas, arboretums and conservatories	Prefabricated shelters	Prefabricated wood trellage and arbors	Shade cloth	Sunrooms
Sunshine Garden House	■		■					■	
Sunshine Rooms			■		■				■
SunTuf		■	■		■				■
Superior Aluminum Products					■				
Texas Greenhouse Co.			■						
Thermal Industries									■
Thermal-Gard			■						■
Timberhouse Post & Beam			■		■				■
Turner Greenhouses			■						
Unicel									■
Universal Forest Products		■							
US Sky/(A Div. of Stora Enterprises Co.)			■		■				■
Vegetable Factory			■						■
Vinyl Tech/PGT									■
Vixen Hill Gazebos		■							
Waldo & Assoc	■		■				■		
Wavecrest Nursery	■	■	■			■	■		
Western Red Cedar Lumber Assn.		■							
Westview Products									■
Wood Innovations of Suffolk						■			

TIP: Cold-climate gardeners get a head start with a cold frame or greenhouse and extend the end of the growing season with row covers.

See Company Index for address and phone information.

Insect Screen
De Witt Co.

Plans for Outdoor Structures
Home Planners

PVC Arbors
DuraVinyl
Stanco Inc.

Shelters and Storage Buildings
Crop King
Handy Home Products
    Shelter King (A Div. of Crop King)

Rough Carpentry

Rustic woods are always a welcome part of gardens. They blend into the surrounding vegetation so that the necessary structures don't stand out to spoil the beauty of the landscape. Natural woods are used most often for staking and support of plants from orchid flower sprays to street trees.

Lodge pole pine tree stakes are the most widely used. Debarked, pressure-treated and whittled to a point on one end, they are very strong and easily pounded into the soil. Lengths can reach nearly twenty feet, but average about eight feet for trees. Lodgepole pine poles are so attractive they are used for creating rustic fences and slats on shade arbors. The natural shape and coloring makes them suitable anywhere from English cottage gardens to Santa Fe courtyards.

The big brother to lodgepole pine is the pressure-treated peeler core. Averaging about ten inches in diameter, they are very strong and make ideal posts for lodgepole arbors. But peelers are available in lengths perfect for heavy arbor beams as well. They make great fence posts because pressure treating greatly enhances resistance to rotting, and they need not be painted or stained either.

Other rustic woods include landscape timbers and railroad ties. Timbers are pressure-treated and smaller, but can be stained or painted. Railroad ties are soaked in creosote. Their dimensions are so stout that they can be stacked like Lincoln logs into easy raised planters with no need for footings or special carpentry.

Bamboo products have long been favored by Japanese gardeners, but Americans are just now discovering its beauty and versatility. Pencil-thin bamboo flower stakes are commonplace, but larger bamboo is growing as a fencing material. All-bamboo fences are labor intensive, but bamboo can be applied to the face of regular wood fences in creative patterns to give the illusion of the Asian fence. Timber bamboo, the largest of all can reach four inches in diameter and thirty feet long, making it a great building material in tropical garden themes. Perhaps most fascinating of all is the Japanese technique of using bamboo as a decorative pipe spillway to feed small water gardens.

Rustic woodwork can make an average landscape positively charming with fences, arbors and even water features. It is also a functional part of young tree support which is essential in areas suffering from high winds. Best of all rustic wood needs no special care and is among the most highly adaptable building material in the garden.

Rough Carpentry

COMPANY	Bamboo	Connectors and fasteners	Lodgepole pine	Lumber	Plastic lumber	Prefabricated wood trellage and arbors	Pressure-treated landscape timbers	Pressure-treated lumber	Railroad ties	Tree stakes
Anderson Design/Garden Arches						■				
Bamboo & Rattan Works	■									■
Bow House/Bowbends						■				
Brojack Lumber Co.							■			
Bufftech						■				
Burton Woodworks (A Div. of MHJ Group)				■		■	■	■		■
Butler Box & Stake	■		■	■						■
California Acrylic Industries/Cal Spas						■				
California Redwood Assn.				■		■				
Century Root Barriers										■
Cepco Tool		■								
Clinton Street Greenhouse										■
Coastal Lumber Co. (Treated Products Div.)							■	■	■	
Crane Plastics Co.					■					
Creative Building Products					■					
Cross Vinylattice						■				
Dalton Pavillions						■				
Earl May Seed & Nursery	■					■				■
Easy Gardener										■
E-Z Deck—Pultronex Corp.					■					
G & R Trellis & Supply Co.	■			■		■	■	■		■
Garden Essence						■				
Genova Products					■					
Gibco Services					■					
Heirloom Seeds						■				
Heritage Vinyl Products						■				
Hoglund Landscape Construction						■	■			
L.B. Plastics					■					
Lee Valley Tools		■								
Mellco					■	■	■	■		
P.L. Rohrer & Bro.						■				
Plastics Research Corp.					■	■				
Plastival					■					
Rahn Trellis Co./(A Div. of MHJ Group)						■				
ReSource Building Products					■					
Select Seeds - Antique Flowers	■									

See Company Index for address and phone information.

Rough Carpentry

COMPANY	Bamboo	Connectors and fasteners	Lodgepole pine	Lumber	Plastic lumber	Prefabricated wood trellage and arbors	Pressure-treated landscape timbers	Pressure-treated lumber	Railroad ties	Tree stakes
Thermal Industries					■					
Waterfall Creations	■									
Wavecrest Nursery						■	■		■	■
Wood Innovations of Suffolk						■				

See Company Index for address and phone information.

TIP: *Proper staking of young saplings with strong supports is the key to a healthy, attractive shade tree many years later.*

Wood Polymer Lumber
Trex Co.

Too much water in the soil is the source of many problems. When it accumulates the soil becomes saturated, and all the air is displaced by water. Like anything else denied air this makes plant roots rot, and plants quickly die. You know when the plant has died of rot when the dead roots come out black and smelling like a sewer. If you put a new plant in the same spot without fixing the problem, it will die the same way.

Drainage is achieved by good grading, but when nature needs help we turn to drainage products. Drain pipe or drain line can be white and rigid like water pipe, requiring special T and elbow fittings to branch off or turn the corner. Since these drainage pipes are not under pressure they don't require the tight fit of pressure lines. Flexible pipes allow you lay the pipe at nearly any alignment you want. They are black, corrugated and less cumbersome options—looking like a giant caterpillar when coiled up.

Drainage pipe can be fed from surface water that enters the system through drop inlets. For an effective system, the surface must be graded so it drains to each inlet. These inlets can be located in raised planters or at grade, and can accommodate a very large volume of water. Each drop inlet is capped with a grate to keep leaves or other material from flowing down inside the system and clogging the pipe.

To drain water trapped underground use a French drain system. This works on the principal that water always moves from an area of greater concentration to one of lesser concentration. A French drain is a piece of perforated pipe laid at the bottom of a trench. It is covered with gravel on all sides, and then the trench is filled in. The water in

Site Improvments

the surrounding soil will naturally travel into the perforated pipe seeking an area of lesser concentration. It then flows down the pipe to another less saturated location.

Many other practical products such as backflow prevention devices are part of the site improvement picture. These allow for storm water, irrigation water and general drainage to function properly so that landscapes large and small can grow to their optimum beauty.

Site Improvements

COMPANY	Backflow prevention devices	Drainage pipe and fittings	Edging and bed dividers	Inlets: trench, gutter, gutter-drop
Argee Corp.			■	
Burton Woodworks (A Div. of MHJ Group)			■	
Clinton Street Greenhouse	■			
Dalen Products			■	
De Witt Co.			■	
Easy Gardener			■	
Flo-Well Water Management		■		
Genova Products		■		
Insulated Building Systems		■		
Laticrete Intl.		■		
Lee Valley Tools			■	
L.M. Scofield Co.		■		
NDS	■	■		■
The Northern Roof Tile Sales Co.			■	
Pave Tech			■	
P.L. Rohrer & Bro.			■	
R & R Products				■
Southern Sales & Marketing Group			■	
Trex Decks			■	
Valley View Industries			■	
Waldo & Assoc	■			
Wavecrest Nursery			■	

> **TIP:** *If you think you have a drainage problem, the only sure way to tell for sure is to dig a hole.*

See Company Index for address and phone information.

Erosion Control
RK Mfg. Grassye Pavers

Filter Fabric
De Witt Co.

Site And Street Furnishings

Site furnishings are the things we use for exterior decorating. These products can be as functional as barbecues, or just pretty like statuary. Either way, when something gets used outdoors it must hold up to the worst punishment conjured up by Mother Nature.

Barbecues can be permanent or portable, use charcoal or propane. Either way the unit must be one that fits the size of your yard and your family. Similarly, your outdoor dining table—be it with individual chairs or a picnic table unit—should be sized for your average number of guests or kids.

All outdoor furniture—from the chaise lounge to the porch swing—must be able to take the wet and the cold. Wood furniture, if it isn't redwood, teak or another very weather-resistant wood, will suffer if left out year around. Wood requires painting or sealing regularly and can be very expensive to buy, particularly fine English and Adirondack style pieces.

Aluminum is costly, but the most popular metal due to its light weight which lets you move it around with ease. Products made with this rust-resistant material also are available in many different colors and patterns, with a variety of accessories as well. Wrought iron is also popular because of its strength and durability, but it can be very hot or cold to sit on in extremes of weather. It can also rust and requires periodic painting, but today's new styles mimic rust and that stylish patina of age without damage.

Planters and pots made of space-age plastics and the original terra cotta are the rage among city gardeners who are now filling balconies and fire escapes with veggies and flowers. Cheaper plastic pots are not worth the money for larger items because they become weakened by ultraviolet light, and the heavy soil mass plus the plant causes them to break if moved around. Buy only high quality UV resistant plastics.

Terra cotta is lovely but fragile and easily cracked or chipped. It can also be very heavy. One of the practical qualities of the plastic pots is that they are water efficient. Clay is so porous and loses moisture through the walls. This not only wastes water in drought-ravaged communities but can cause discoloration on the outside—some people love this and others don't.

Art for the garden is everywhere, with something that appeals to everyone's personal idea of beauty. Always view art in the garden context, not as something that is merely appealing, because once in the landscape it may turn tacky. Today's finishes for birdbaths, statuary and other concrete objects mimic copper verdigris, bronze and dark stone, so don't settle for the old white-washed piece. Remember, you'll have to live with it for a very long time.

When buying outdoor furniture, art, containers and other pricy items, always lean toward the higher-quality products. If you compromise and buy the cheap one, consider its original price plus that of the new one to find out if you really saved money in the long run.

Site And Street Furnishings

COMPANY	Barbecue units	Benches	Campfire pits	Deck accessories	Decking	Flagpoles	Footbridges	Garden art and statuary	Garden furniture	Mailboxes	Picnic tables	Prefabricated decorative planters and pots	Prefabricated shelters	Signage	Spas and accessories	Tree grates	Trim/lattice	Vinyl decking/membrane	Waste receptacles
Almost Heaven				■											■		■		
Alsto's Handy Helpers		■						■	■			■							
Anchor Decking Systems																		■	
Aqua Plunge/Aqua Plunge Div.															■				
Aquatic Industries															■				
Aristech Acrylics															■				
The Astrup Co.													■						
Austram												■							
Avva Light Corp.														■					
Baja Products															■				
Baker Mfg. Corp.															■				
Beacon Products		■								■				■					
Belson Outdoors	■	■	■								■								■
Berry Hill Limited	■					■		■											
Bosmere									■										
Boston Design Corp.									■	■									■
Bow House/Bowbends							■						■						
Brandon Industries										■				■					
Brite Millwork				■													■		
Brochure Box Co.										■				■					
Brock Deck Systems/Royal Crown Ltd.					■												■	■	
Bufftech		■								■									
Burton Woodworks (A Div. of MHJ Group)		■															■		
Butler Box & Stake									■										
Caldera Spas & Baths															■				
California Acrylic Industries/Cal Spas	■									■		■			■				
California Redwood Assn.		■								■	■	■							
Cangelosi Marble and Granite														■					
Canital Granite														■					
Cepco Tool				■															
CertainTeed Corp. Pipe & Plastics Group										■							■	■	
Classic Lamp Posts										■									
Coastal Lumber Co./(Treated Products Div.)				■													■		
Concrete Designs		■										■							■
Country Casual		■							■										■
Crane Plastics Co.					■													■	

See Company Index for address and phone information.

COMPANY	Barbecue units	Benches	Campfire pits	Deck accessories	Decking	Flagpoles	Footbridges	Garden art and statuary	Garden furniture	Mailboxes	Picnic tables	Prefabricated decorative planters and pots	Prefabricated shelters	Signage	Spas and accessories	Tree grates	Trim/lattice	Vinyl decking/membrane	Waste receptacles
Creative Building Products				■													■		
Crop King													■						
Cross Vinylattice																	■		
Cumberland Woodcraft									■										
Curt Bean Lumber Co.				■													■		
Dakota Granite														■					
Dalton Pavillions													■						
David Bacon Fine Handcrafted Furniture												■							
Davidson Wilson Greenhouses	■		■																
Day-Dex Co.		■																	
DEC-K-ING				■	■													■	
DecTec				■														■	
Dee Sign Co.														■					
Desertland Nursery		■						■				■							
DM Industries/Vita Intl.															■				
Earl May Seed & Nursery								■											
Elements										■				■					
Ensurco Duradek (U.S.)					■													■	
E-Z Deck—Pultronex Corp.					■														
Fiberglass Access															■				
Forms + Surfaces							■												
FSI Home Products Div./Flotation Systems					■														
Fypon														■			■		
Gerber Industries				■															
Grabber Construction Products				■															
Great Southern Wood Preserving					■					■							■		
Greenheart-Durawoods					■														
Haddonstone (USA)								■				■							
Hanover Lantern										■									
Heritage Vinyl Products										■	■						■	■	
Herwig Lighting										■									
Hoglund Landscape Construction		■				■		■	■			■							
Idaho Wood										■									
International Cast Polymer Assn.															■				
Jacuzzi Whirlpool Bath															■				
Jancik Arts								■						■					
Kodiak					■												■		
Kroy Building Products										■	■							■	
Kuny's Mfg. Co.				■															
Landscape Structures										■				■					■
L.B. Plastics				■														■	
Lee Valley Tools						■				■				■					
Liberty Seed Co.						■		■		■									
Lowen Sign Co.														■					
MAAX/Div. Acrylica, Premium															■				
Mansfield Plumbing Products															■				
Marathon Spa & Bath															■				
Marell Industries										■				■					
Marketshare														■					
Mary's Plant Farm								■				■							
Masco Corp.															■				
Mel Northey Co.										■									
Mellco				■	■					■							■		

See Company Index for address and phone information.

Company	Barbecue units	Benches	Campfire pits	Deck accessories	Decking	Flagpoles	Footbridges	Garden art and statuary	Garden furniture	Mailboxes	Picnic tables	Prefabricated decorative planters and pots	Prefabricated shelters	Signage	Spas and accessories	Tree grates	Trim/lattice	Vinyl decking/membrane	Waste receptacles
Moultrie Mfg.									■	■									
MTC (Media Trade Corp.)										■									
National Spa and Pool Institute															■				
NDS																■			
Neenah Foundry Co.																■			
Old Strathcona Garden Shoppe								■	■			■							
Out of the Redwoods												■							
Park Place		■							■			■							■
Permalatt																	■		
Philstone Fasteners				■															
P.L. Rohrer & Bro.						■		■											
Plastics Research Corp.				■													■		
Plastival					■												■		
Plumbing Manufacturers Institute														■					
Pompeian Studios								■	■										
Prudential Building Materials					■												■		
PS Aluminum Products					■														
Quarry Tile Co.														■					
Quick Crete Products Corp.	■	■	■							■		■		■		■			■
R & R Products		■		■										■					■
Renato Bisazza														■					
ReSource Building Products																		■	
Rio Plastics															■				
Rotocast/Terracast												■							
Ryan Forest Products					■												■		
Sarnafil					■														
Scott Sign Systems														■					
Seton Identification Products														■					
Signs by Mayo														■					
Sitecraft Corp.				■					■										
Smart Deck Systems					■														
SNOC										■									
Snorkel Stove Co.															■				
Southeast Wood					■												■		
Southern Pine Council				■															
Southern Sales & Marketing Group					■														
Southland Spa & Sauna															■				
SouthWood Corp.														■					
Spiral Stairs of America				■															
St. Thomas Creations															■				
Stanco Inc.		■									■	■							
Steel & Wire Products Co.																	■		
Stone Forest		■					■	■	■										
Stonewear, Inc.		■									■	■							■
Straubel Stone Lightweight	■																		
Sun Garden Specialities		■						■	■					■					
Sunesta Products					■														
Sunset Moulding Co.																	■		
Supreme Decking					■														
SwimEx Systems															■				
TR Miller Mill Co.																	■		
Treessentials Co.																■			
Trex Co.				■	■														

See Company Index for address and phone information.

COMPANY	Barbecue units	Benches	Campfire pits	Deck accessories	Decking	Flagpoles	Footbridges	Garden art and statuary	Garden furniture	Mailboxes	Picnic tables	Prefabricated decorative planters and pots	Prefabricated shelters	Signage	Spas and accessories	Tree grates	Trim/lattice	Vinyl decking/membrane	Waste receptacles
Triple Crown Fence/Royal Crown Ltd.					■												■	■	
Tubco Whirlpools															■				
Universal Forest Products					■												■	■	
Valley View Industries												■							
Versadek Industries																		■	
Waldo & Assoc												■							
Waterfall Creations							■	■											
Watertech															■				
Wausau Tile														■					
Wavecrest Nursery	■	■	■				■	■	■		■				■	■			■
Wellington Leisure Products							■												
Western Red Cedar Lumber Assn.				■													■		
White Flower Farm								■				■							
Wikco Industries		■																	
Wind and Weather		■						■	■										

TIP: *Anything you use outdoors must be of the highest quality if it is to survive the rigors of weather.*

See Company Index for address and phone information.

Curved and Spiral Stairs
Spiral Stairs of America

Custom Precast Furnishings
Quick Crete Products Corp.

Deck Railings
DecTec
Feeney Wire Rope & Rigging

Docks
Thermal Industries

Garden Ornaments
Stone Forest

Mailbox Posts
Burton Woodworks (A Div. of
    MHJ Group)
The Gordon Corp.

Metal Arbors and Trellises
Mary's Plant Farm

Patio Heaters
Garland Commercial
    Industries

Plant Stands
The Violet House

Precast Furniture
Wausau Tile

Soil Preparation

If there's one thing you have to get right with gardening, it's soil preparation. Let's face it, nobody has perfect dirt. Every soil can benefit from enhancement by organic matter. However, organic matter alone is not what makes a soil fertile. It needs humus, which is partially decomposed organic matter that's immediately available for plants.

The cheapest source of humus comes from your own kitchen and garden in the form of compost. Organic refuse gathered and layered becomes a hotbed of microorganisms. When these are transferred to your soil through finished compost, the plants get a great long-term feast and will reward you in kind.

Making compost is easy if you use one of the many bins on the market today. They help speed up the process, keep the material in a tidy space and make it less attractive to foraging pets and wildlife. Most are designed to make the process of stirring compost easier. You can shovel them out from the bottom without opening up the bin. Another product of interest to composting is compost booster that introduces microorganisms to your heap to speed up the decomposition process.

There is a huge market of fertilizers out there, the bulkiest being the organic products such as bagged manures, ready-made compost and a variety of animal, vegetable and mineral byproducts. Although slower to act, these products work for a long time, enhancing soil fertility and providing essential micro-nutrients for a balanced, active organic soil.

Inorganic fertilizers are powerful chemicals that are immediately available to plants. Liquid and granular products are formulated for lawns, roses, vegetables and acid-loving plants. They do not offer much in the way of organic matter and micro-nutrients, but are great time and money savers for home gardeners. Always look for the N-P-K on the label which indicates the percentages of nitrogen, phosphorus and potassium the fertilizer contains. Like food products you can compare package weight and nutrient percentages to get the best deal.

The geotextile industry has produced a great labor saving device called weed barrier fabric. It replaces the old black plastic sheeting popular in the 1960s, which had lots of problems and cut off oxygen and water to plant roots. Weed fabric is unique in that it is woven, allowing air and water exchanges to take place, but blocks all light so that weed seedlings never see the sun. Long lasting, easy to work with and widely available, weed fabric allows you to plant through it successfully and cover it up with more attractive ground bark or gravel mulches.

Never forget that the soil is the most fundamental part of the garden. It needs to be renewed so that as plants consume nutrients they are replaced at an equal rate. Whether you choose to garden organically or with the labor-saving benefits of modern science, keep one eye on the ground at all times and treasure your soil like a precious family heirloom.

Soil Preparation

COMPANY	Compost bins and accessories	Erosion control mats and nets	Organic gardening products	Root feeders and fertilizer application tools	Soil conditioners/fertilizers	Topsoil	Weed barrier fabrics											
A-1 Unique Insect Control			■															
Age-Old Organics			■															
American Arborist Supplies					■													
Amerigrow Recycling			■		■													
Bear Creek Nursery			■	■														
Bio-Gard Agronomics			■															
Bonide Products			■															
Bronwood Worm Farms	■		■															
Broyhill				■			■											
Burlington Scientific Corp.			■		■													
Cape Cod Worm Farm			■		■													
Century Root Barriers				■			■											
Chas. C. Hart Seed Co.		■			■		■											
Clinton Street Greenhouse						■	■											
Colorblends by Schipper & Co.			■															
Crop King	■		■	■	■	■	■											
Dalen Products							■											
Davidson Wilson Greenhouses	■		■	■	■	■	■											
De Witt Co.							■											
Dramm Corporation			■															
Dyna-Gro Nutrition Solutions				■	■													
Earl May Seed & Nursery			■	■	■	■	■											
Easy Gardener		■		■	■		■											
Farm Wholesale Greenhouses		■	■															
Florida Mycology Research Center			■															
Florikan Southeast					■		■											
Fox Hill Nursery					■													
Garden of Delights		■	■		■		■											
Gourmet Mushroom Products	■																	
The Green Escape			■	■	■													
The Guano Co. Intl.			■															
Heirloom Seeds			■				■											
Hoglund Landscape Construction							■											
Hy Grade Planting Mix			■		■	■												
Hydro Turf				■														
Integrated Fertiltiy Management			■		■		■											

See Company Index for address and phone information.

COMPANY	Compost bins and accessories	Erosion control mats and nets	Organic gardening products	Root feeders and fertilizer application tools	Soil conditioners/fertilizers	Topsoil	Weed barrier fabrics
John Deere Consumer Equip. Div.				■			
Johnson Nursery			■	■	■	■	■
Karl Kuemmerling, Inc.				■			
L & L Nursery Supply			■	■	■	■	
Lee Valley Tools	■		■	■			■
Liberty Seed Co.			■		■		■
Morco Products	■						
Mushroom People			■				
Nature's Control			■				
NDS							■
Necessary Organics			■		■		
Nedia Enterprises		■	■		■		■
Nitron Industries	■		■		■		
Northwind Nursery and Orchards	■		■		■		
Ohio Earth Food			■				
Old Strathcona Garden Shoppe			■				
Pacific Tree Farms			■				
Pinetree Garden Seeds	■		■		■		■
P.L. Rohrer & Bro.		■		■	■	■	■
Planet Natural	■		■				
Prairie Ridge Nursery/CRM Ecosystems, Inc.		■					
Premier Environmental Products					■		
Reemay							■
RK Mfg. Grassye Pavers		■					
Rod McLellan Co.					■	■	
RoLanka Intl.		■					
Sea Born/Lane			■		■		
Select Seeds - Antique Flowers			■		■		
Shelter King (A Div. of Crop King)	■						
Shepard's Garden Seeds	■		■				
Soils Plus Recycling					■	■	
Solarcone	■						
Southern Barks			■				
Stanco Inc.	■						
Superthrive					■		
Tree Pro					■		■
Treessentials Co.				■			
Waldo & Assoc					■		■
Wavecrest Nursery		■	■		■	■	■

See Company Index for address and phone information.

TIP: *High quality organic soil is alive with microorganisms that help plants grow fast and resist pests naturally.*

Barrier Weed Control
Hoglund Landscape
   Construction

Compost Activator
Necessary Organics

Compost Thermometers
Reo Temp Instrument Corp.

Earthworms
A-1 Unique Insect Control
Bronwood Worm Farms
Cape Cod Worm Farm
Mother Nature's Worm
   Castings

Moisture Meters
Reo Temp Instrument Corp.

Perlite
Perlite of Texas

Soil Meters
D.V. Burrell Seed Growers
Co.

Stone is timeless and represents the permanence of earth. It tends to represent different regions of our nation with bluestone in New England and pink sandstone of Arizona. Heavy and expensive to transport, it is becoming one of the more rare elements in landscaping.

But for landscaping au naturel, there is nothing like a weathered, lichen-encrusted mossy boulder to anchor planting. These can be expensive if there is no natural source nearby. Japanese gardeners are consummate boulder users and are very picky about each stone they use. You have the right to be just as choosey and should never buy one sight unseen.

River cobbles are simply those lovely rounded rocks that fill stream beds. They make excellent accents and are used as a stone mulch over landscape fabric. Because they are round, cobbles are not well suited for rock walls and other garden construction.

Rubble stone, on the other hand is sharp and irregular, salvaged from both demolished buildings and where field stone accumulations occur naturally. This angular quality makes them good for dry stone walls and those using concrete or mortar. They also make fine pilasters and gateways.

Cut or hewed stone is also expensive due to the labor to shape it. These units are most versatile and may be used for decorative posts, benches, curbs and stacked walls. Flatter slate-like stone is

Stone

easy to work with and is cherished by rock gardeners and for stepping stones.

Above all, it is the transport and placement of stone that is costly. Shipping even short distances demands flat-bed trucks and trailers. Boulders cannot be easily moved or placed by hand so heavy equipment is required. Fortunately you need only haul and place stone once, for its life span is infinite and will be forever a part of your garden.

Stone

COMPANY	PRODUCTS																			
	Cut stone	Landscape boulders	River cobble	Rubble stone																
Cangelosi Marble and Granite	■																			
Clinton Street Greenhouse	■	■																		
Earl May Seed & Nursery		■																		
Grani-Decor Tiles	■																			
Hoglund Landscape Construction		■																		
Maine Millstones	■																			
Petmal Supply Co.	■		■	■																
P.L. Rohrer & Bro.		■	■																	
Rocktile Specialty Products	■																			
Stone Forest	■																			
Wavecrest Nursery	■	■																		

> **TIP:** *Always "plant" your landscape boulders a few inches into the ground to make them look more natural.*

See Company Index for address and phone information.

Carved Stone
Sun Garden Specialities

Cast Stone
Haddonstone (USA)
Straubel Stone Lightweight

Crushed Stone
London Tile Co.

Veneer Stone
Cultured Stone Corp.
Rocktile Specialty Products

Trees, Plants And Groundcovers

When you buy a plant, you buy a life. Whether it is sequestered inside a tiny seed or bursting out like a hot-house orchid, all plants are alive. This is what separates them from the rest of the gardening world composed of more practical objects such as tools or sprinklers.

The companies in this section do business in different ways. Some have retail stores that you must visit or at least call for information. Many are strictly mail order and offer extensive catalogs for you to browse through conveniently without ever leaving home. These companies ship plants to you during the appropriate season of the year for your immediate climate.

Many mail-order growers offer a much wider assortment to choose from because they do business directly with you. Mail order is not only convenient, it allows you to choose from a vast array of less common varieties rarely carried at retail nurseries. This is a benefit to advanced gardeners who are plant collectors or to anyone who feels like experimenting outside the realm of the tried and true.

Plants are sold in a variety of ways, and buying by mail does have its limitations. While seeds are the very best item to order by mail, fleshy perennial plants may appear disappointing compared to the glorious color pictures in the catalogs. It's hard to ship a good-sized plant without damage, and during the growing season, you may be able to find a much bigger specimen for less money at home improvement stores.

Here's what you can expect from the mail order companies' products:

■ Seeds are the best value because they ship easily and aren't bulky or heavy. Buy fresh seeds each season to ensure you have good germination rates and healthy plants.

■ Perennials are sold either as bare-root cuttings or divisions. They can also be shipped in little containers depending on the grower. With so many great flowers out there, you'll be able to start uncommon plants that can be divided up in future years.

■ Roses are sold bare root during the dormant season. With hundreds of varieties on the market, catalog shopping is a better option than buying retail, particularly when seeking old-fashioned varieties.

■ Fruit trees and berry bushes are bare-root stock and sold by catalog from some of America's best companies. The selection is enormous and you benefit from the growing advice offered by those companies which is crucial to the ability of the plant to remain hardy and produce a crop in your climate.

■ Deciduous ornamental trees and shrubs are sold bare root or in small containers depending on the source. However, local retailers will beat the size and price for most ordinary varieties.

Whether you're looking for a certain water lily, tropical plants, cacti or Grandmother's old rose, it's here among these specialty growers. America's nursery industry offers practically every plant in cultivation. The trick is to decide what company is right for you and your garden.

Trees, Plants And Groundcovers

PRODUCTS

COMPANY	Aquatics	Bulbs	Cacti and succulents	Daylilies	Edible plants	Ferns	Groundcovers	Herbs	Hostas	Irises	Native plants	Orchids	Perennials	Roses	Seed sources	Seeds—cover crops	Seeds—edible plants	Seeds—grass	Seeds—pastures	Seeds—wildflowers	Shrubs—subtropic	Shrubs—temperate	Trees—conifers	Trees—shade, flowery, fruit	Tropical and greenhouse plants	Vines
Abundant Life Seed Foundation																■	■			■				■	■	
Adventures in Herbs							■	■																		
Air Expose																										
Allen Plant Co.					■																					
Alpine Gardens							■																			
American Willow Growers Network																						■				
Ann Mann's Orchids												■														■
Appalachian Gardens																						■	■	■		
Bark Plus																		■								
Barney's Ginseng Patch								■					■							■						
Barth Daylilies				■																						
Bear Creek Nursery		■					■							■			■					■		■		■
Bird Rock Tropicals												■													■	
Bloomingfields Farm				■			■						■													
Bluestem Prairie Nursery																				■						
Borbeleta Gardens		■											■													
Bountiful Gardens								■								■	■	■								
Brent and Becky's Bulbs		■																								
The Bulb Crate		■																								
Burnt Ridge Nursery						■																		■		■
Busse Gardens						■	■																			
Butterbrooke Farm																						■				
Cactus by Dodie			■																							
Caladium World		■																								
Callahan Seeds							■															■	■	■	■	
Camellia Forest Nursery																						■	■	■		■
Campberry Farms																							■			
Canadian Wildflower Society	■	■					■	■			■		■		■				■	■		■	■	■		
Cape Iris Gardens		■		■						■			■													
Carino Nurseries																							■	■	■	
Carlson's Garden's																						■				
Carmel Valley Seed Co.																				■						
Cascade Forest Nursery																							■	■		
Chas. C. Hart Seed Co.																		■								
Clargreen Gardens	■	■					■	■					■	■				■				■		■	■	■
Clinton Street Greenhouse							■	■					■	■				■							■	■

See Company Index for address and phone information.

PRODUCTS

Company	Aquatics	Bulbs	Cacti and succulents	Daylilies	Edible plants	Ferns	Groundcovers	Herbs	Hostas	Irises	Native plants	Orchids	Perennials	Roses	Seed sources	Seeds—cover crops	Seeds—edible plants	Seeds—grass	Seeds—pastures	Seeds—wildflowers	Shrubs—subtropic	Shrubs—temperate	Trees—conifers	Trees—shade, flowery, fruit	Tropical and greenhouse plants	Vines
Cloud Forest Orchids																									■	
Cold Stream Farm											■											■	■	■		■
Colorblends by Schipper & Co.		■																■								
Colvos Creek Nursery							■						■									■	■	■		■
Comanche Acres Iris Gardens										■																
Companion Plants								■			■		■				■			■				■		
Comstock Seed																■	■	■	■	■						
The Conservancy															■					■						
Cooley's Strawberry Nursery					■																					
Crop King					■		■									■						■	■	■		■
Crosman Seed Corp.							■										■	■		■						
Cummins Garden							■						■									■	■			
The Daffodil Mart		■																								
Davidson Wilson Greenhouses		■				■	■	■					■				■	■		■					■	
Daylily Discounters							■						■													
DeGiorgi Seed Co.								■									■	■		■						
Desertland Nursery			■												■											
Donovan's Roses														■												
Dutch Gardens		■											■													
J.V. Burrell Seed Growers Co.								■								■	■			■						
Earl May Seed & Nursery	■	■					■						■	■		■	■	■	■	■		■	■	■	■	■
Earthly Goods															■					■						
Edible Landscaping							■							■			■					■	■	■		■
Elixir Farm Botanicals								■																		
Fancy Fronds						■																				
Fieldstone Gardens						■	■						■													■
Flickinger's Nursery							■																■			
Florida Colors Nursery																								■	■	
Florida Mycology Research Center																					■					
Forestfarm						■	■				■		■									■	■	■		■
ForestLake Gardens				■																						
Fox Hill Nursery														■												
Fred's Plant Farm																										■
Freshops																										■
Frey's Dahlias		■																								
Friendship Gardens									■	■			■													
Frosty Holly Ecological Restoration											■						■			■						
Garden of Delights				■											■		■					■		■	■	■
Garden Perennials													■													
Garden Place													■													
Gardens of the Blue Ridge						■	■						■							■				■		■
Gilbert H. Wild and Son													■													
Golden Lake Greenhouses																									■	
Good Seed Co.		■													■		■			■						
Goodwin Creek Gardens							■	■					■				■			■		■		■		■
Gossler Farms Nursery																						■		■		
The Gourmet Gardener		■											■				■									
The Green Escape																							■		■	
Greenthumb Daylily Gardens				■					■	■																
Hood Seed Co.		■													■		■			■						
Grimo Nut Nursery																								■		
Hauser's Superior View Farm							■						■													
Heaths and Heathers																						■				

See Company Index for address and phone information.

PRODUCTS

Company	Aquatics	Bulbs	Cacti and succulents	Daylilies	Edible plants	Ferns	Groundcovers	Herbs	Hostas	Irises	Native plants	Orchids	Perennials	Roses	Seed sources	Seeds—cover crops	Seeds—edible plants	Seeds—grass	Seeds—pastures	Seeds—wildflowers	Shrubs—subtropic	Shrubs—temperate	Trees—conifers	Trees—shade, flowery, fruit	Tropical and greenhouse plants	Vines
Heirloom Seeds								●									●									
Hidden Springs Nursery																						●		●		
Hildebrandt's Gardens		●					●						●													
Hillary's Garden							●																			
Historical Roses														●												
Holland Bulb Farms		●																								
Holland Gardens										●																
Holland Wildflower Farm						●	●						●	●	●				●	●						●
Homestead Farms				●			●		●				●									●		●		
Hughes Nursery																						●		●		
IntAgra Deer-away																	●									
Integrated Fertiltiy Management																●			●							
International Oleander Society																					●	●				
Iris & Plus													●													
Isabel Hibbard Gardens													●													
J & L Orchids												●														
Jerry Horne Rare Plants						●																			●	
John Gordon Nursery																								●		
Johnny's Selected Seeds													●		●	●	●			●						
Johnson Daylily Garden				●																						
Johnson Nursery		●				●	●						●	●			●			●				●		
Kasch Nursery																				●			●			
Kay's Greenhouses													●													
Kester's Wild Game Food Nurseries											●															
Kirkland Daylilies				●																						
Kuk's Forest Nursery									●				●													
L & L Nursery Supply																					●					
Ladybug Daylilies				●																						
Larner Seeds																		●		●						
Lee Gardens						●	●						●													
Lee's Botanical Garden	●	●				●						●													●	●
Lewis Mountain Herbs & Everlastings								●																		
Liberty Seed Co.							●						●				●			●						
Lily of the Valley Herb Farm	●					●	●	●					●	●											●	●
Living Stones Nursery			●																	●						
Lon J. Rombough					●																					
Mary's Plant Farm	●	●				●	●	●					●	●						●		●	●	●	●	●
Mendocino Heirloom Roses														●												
Miami Water Lilies	●																								●	
Mid-America Garden													●													
Midwest Cactus			●										●													
Midwest Wildflowers																				●						
Moon Mountain Wildflowers																●				●						
Mountain Valley Growers							●	●					●	●											●	
Native Gardens						●	●				●		●							●		●				
Native Seeds																				●						
Nature's Garden			●			●	●						●													
New England Wild Flower Society						●														●						
Northern Kiwi Nursery																								●		●
Northplan/Mountain Seed															●	●	●	●	●	●			●	●		●
Northridge Gardens		●	●										●									●	●		●	●
Northwind Nursery and Orchards																								●		●
Nourse Farms					●																					

See Company Index for address and phone information.

PRODUCTS

COMPANY	Aquatics	Bulbs	Cacti and succulents	Daylilies	Edible plants	Ferns	Groundcovers	Herbs	Hostas	Irises	Native plants	Orchids	Perennials	Roses	Seed sources	Seeds—cover crops	Seeds—edible plants	Seeds—grass	Seeds—pastures	Seeds—wildflowers	Shrubs—subtropic	Shrubs—temperate	Trees—conifers	Trees—shade, flowery, fruit	Tropical and greenhouse plants	Vines
rseries at North Glen																									■	
kes Daylilies				■																						
kridge Nursery	■	■				■	■						■													
llie Daylilies Gardens					■								■													
House Gardens		■																								
Strathcona Garden Shoppe		■					■						■	■	■		■	■		■		■				■
gon Trail Daffodils		■																								
cific Tree Farms													■									■	■	■	■	■
mpered Plant Nursery																									■	
radise Water Gardens	■																									
nse Nursery						■											■								■	
e Pepper Gal													■													
eapple Place																									■	
necliffe Daylily Gardens				■					■				■													
netree Garden Seeds		■					■						■			■	■			■						
. Rohrer & Bro.		■														■	■	■	■	■						
ntasia Cactus Gardens			■																							
nt Delights Nursery	■					■	■						■										■			
nts of the Wild							■				■					■	■			■		■	■			■
airie Moon Nursery											■							■		■						
airie Ridge Nursery/CRM Ecosystems, Inc.																■		■		■						
att's Power Equipment													■													
entiss Court Ground Covers							■																			
sland Farm						■																				
d's Rhodies		■										■	■												■	
e Reveg Edge																	■									
verdale Iris Gardens										■			■													
d McLellan Co.												■														
s-Equus		■												■												
ses of Yesterday & Today														■												
ses Unlimited														■												
Seawright Gardens				■					■																	
& S Seeds																		■		■						
t Spring Seeds																■	■			■						
ndy Mush Herb Nursery						■	■	■			■		■				■						■	■	■	■
xton Gardens				■									■													
hlabach's Nursery																								■		■
hreiner's Iris Gardens													■													
eds Trust: High Altitude Gardens																■	■	■	■	■						
lect Seeds - Antique Flowers													■		■											■
rra Gardens Cacti & Succulents			■																							
ady Oaks Nursery						■	■						■													
ein's Cactus			■																							
epard Iris Garden										■																
epherd's Garden Seeds							■										■			■						
ooting Star Nursery	■					■	■						■									■	■			■
ver Springs Nursery						■	■				■															
Williams Gardens													■													
cum Water Gardens	■																									
noma Grapevines					■																					■
ules Garden				■					■																	
ruce Gardens		■								■																
ock Seed Farms																■		■	■	■						

■ Company index for address and phone information.

Trees, Plants And Groundcovers

PRODUCTS

COMPANY	Aquatics	Bulbs	Cacti and succulents	Daylilies	Edible plants	Ferns	Groundcovers	Herbs	Hostas	Irises	Native plants	Orchids	Perennials	Roses	Seed sources	Seeds—cover crops	Seeds—edible plants	Seeds—grass	Seeds—pastures	Seeds—wildflowers	Shrubs—subtropic	Shrubs—temperate	Trees—conifers	Trees—shade, flowery, fruit	Tropical and greenhouse plants	Vines
Sunrise Nursery			■																						■	
Sunshine Farm & Gardens	■	■				■	■						■	■										■		■
Swanns' Daylily Garden				■																						
Thundering Springs Daylily Garden				■					■				■													
Tilley's Nursery/The Waterworks	■																									
The Urban Homestead																								■		
Van Bourgondien Bros.		■					■		■				■													■
Van Dyke Zinnias/@ Redbud Farms																■	■									
Van Ness Water Gardens	■																									
Van Well Nursery																								■		
Vernon Barns & Son Nursery						■	■		■				■											■		■
Vesey's Seeds		■														■	■	■								
Vileniki—An Herb Farm						■	■	■					■													■
The Violet House													■													
Waterfall Creations	■																									
Wavecrest Nursery	■	■				■	■						■				■			■		■	■	■	■	■
We-Du Nursery	■	■				■	■						■											■		
White Flower Farm		■				■	■						■	■								■		■	■	■
White Oak Nursery									■																	
Wildflower Nursery	■	■				■	■				■		■									■				■
The Wildflower Seed Co.																				■						
Wildseed Farms																				■						
Wildwood Gardens	■	■					■													■						
Willhite Seed																	■									
William Dam Seeds																■	■	■		■						
Willow Oak Flower & Herb Farm								■					■	■			■			■		■				
Windrose												■	■										■	■	■	■
Winn Soldani's Fancy Hibiscus																									■	
Wood Prairie Farm																	■									
Woodlanders	■	■				■	■						■									■	■	■	■	■

See Company Index for address and phone information.

Azaleas
Carlson's Garden's
Cummins Garden
Nuccio's Nurseries

Camelias
Nuccio's Nurseries

Carnivorous Plants
Lee's Botanical Garden
Peter Pauls Nurseries

Flower Patch Kits
Ampro Industries

Lilacs
Fox Hill Nursery

Mushrooms
Field and Forest Products
Florida Mycology Research Center
Gourmet Mushroom Products
Hardscrabble Enterprises
Mushroompeople

Seeds—Jojoba
KSA Jojoba

Seeds—Variety
P & P Seed Co.
Thompson and Morgan Inc.

Sphagnum Moss
Peter Pauls Nurseries

Wildflowers
Bluestem Prairie Nursery
Oakridge Nursery

Willow Cuttings
American Willow Growers Network

Walk, Road And Parking Appurtunances

When you want to control vehicles, you need to tell them where to go. For bicycles it's a safe parking zone that allows the bikes to be padlocked so they're still around when you return. At home, bike racks also keep the kid's toys off the driveway, patio and lawn.

Bollards are primarily motor-vehicle oriented. They above all serve as barriers to exclude autos while allowing pedestrians and bicycles free access. They are also good at keeping cars off lawns and visually identifying parking areas.

Bollard style should match the character of the landscape or adjacent building. You can get Nineteenth-

Century cast iron types that are highly ornamental and may be painted any color that's appropriate. Slick modern designs fit contemporary architecture and may be constructed out of wood, steel or concrete.

Bollards can be lighted serving as safety elements as well as barriers. Though expensive and manufactured for institutional use, lighted bollards can be excellent problem solvers for larger residential homesites.

Keep in mind that bollards are expensive no matter what the scale, and if lighted the price jumps considerably. But, unlike bicycle racks which only challenge thieves, bollards must be strong enough to take on the mighty automobile.

Walk, Road And Parking Appurtenances

COMPANY	300100 bicycle racks	300150 bollards
Belson Outdoors	■	
Landscape Structures	■	
Stonewear, Inc.		■
U.S. Gaslight		■
Wavecrest Nursery	■	

See Company Index for address and phone information.

Parking Surfaces
RK Mfg. Grassye Pavers

Landscapes

Can You Dig 'Em?

Borders of colorful blooms delight young and old alike.

Professional landscaping is an important part of your home. It provides an extension of interior rooms and quiet pockets of nature that soothe irritated nerves and calm a troubled spirit. As if that's not enough, consider the added value that beautiful landscaping contributes to your home. From bodacious borders to the naturalistic wonders of nature, your landscape can introduce you to a colorful piece of the outdoors that awaits the special magic created by your green thumb.

Landscape Planning

First of all, you'll want to investigate landscaping possibilities. Talk with friends, relatives and neighbors who have installed landscapes. Ask about their landscaping experiences and why they made their particular choices. Ask what they would have done differently and what they are most pleased with. Find out how they accomplished the projects—did they contract them out or do the work themselves.

Finally, use your own imagination, combining what you've seen, heard and read about gardening and outdoor plans, to devise the landscape that best suits your home, your family and your lifestyle. Take into account how you will use your yard area. Do you entertain often? Formally or informally? Do you have small children whose needs must be accommodated in the yard area? Do you want a spa or hot tub addition? Will you want to build a pool in the yard at some point in the future? Do you prefer a formal-looking yard or one that's more casual? What style of house do you have? Do you enjoy gardening or would you rather have an easy-care landscape? The answers to these questions will put you on the path to finding the landscape that is right for you.

Even small areas are easily dressed up with the proper combination of flowers and shrubs.

Landscapes

Trees lend beauty as well as welcome shade when combined with colorful groundcover & shrubs.

Groundcover provides a quiet riot of color that complements tall stalks of gladiolas mixed with the vibrant landscape.

Backyard Landscapes

Backyards are more inconspicuous than front yards and consequently can be less dependent on the style of your home and those in the neighborhood. However, there are other considerations that must be taken into account. For instance, backyards are usually the main outdoor areas for recreation, hobbies, entertaining, and fruit and vegetable gardening. Depending on your personal lifestyle and the needs of your family, there are elements you will want to incorporate. Several of the amenities listed below will enhance your beautiful new landscape. Some of these include:

- Storage sheds, small barns or garages for storing gardening equipment
- Gazebos or arbors for privacy areas or entertaining
- Whirlpool or swimming pool
- Play areas such as sports courts and play structures
- Protected areas for food or flower gardening and compost bins
- Designated areas for pets such as kennels or dog runs
- Deck, patio or terrace areas for sunning, relaxing and entertaining

A useful backyard will include all of the items that make it a practical and inviting area for all members of the family without being a burden to maintain.

Front-Yard Landscapes

Landscapes, like any other home amenity, look best if they fit the house they surround. You'll want a front-yard landscape plan that complements and enhances the style of your home while fitting in well with the other homes in your neighborhood. For example: If you have a very traditional home, you'll want a plan that is stately and formal looking. A low-slung ranch house might look best with an informal rustic landscape. Other factors to think about:

- *Climate in your area*
  You'll want to choose plants and trees that thrive in your climate.
- *Topography of your lot*
  You'll need to work around slopes and other irregularities.
- *Use of your front yard*
  Will your front yard be used as an outdoor gathering place or is it mainly just "for show?"
- *Degree of maintenance*
  Do you love to work in the yard or

A stone walkway lends charm to a picturesque cottage garden brightened by tulips.

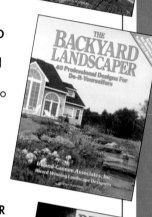

are you a reluctant gardener?

Do-It-Yourself or Contract Out?

The final question is, do I want to do-it-myself or contract out? The answer—if you are fairly well-versed in gardening and building, you may be quite comfortable with doing things yourself. If you don't enjoy do-it-yourself projects, why torture yourself into thinking you want to take one on? Leave it to the professionals and enjoy the finished product knowing you didn't spend your valuable time and energy on something you hated to do. Ultimately, the reward is the same; the feeling of satisfaction that comes from making the outside of your home as comfortable and handsome as the inside. Just select your favorite landscape plan from the following pages and dig in!

Traditional One-Story Home

This classic house style, with its steep roofline and tidy clapboards, demands a traditional, shade-tree-filled landscape. Fulfilling that function is a trio of elegant branching deciduous trees. A specimen tree in the foundation planting on the left of the house provides dramatic spring blossoms and summer shade.

The trees and shrubs in the beds are underplanted with groundcovers, perennials, and bulbs. All the plants in the design were chosen for ease of care and for their attractive foliage, flowers, or fruit. For instance, the clusters of tough bronze-leaved shrubs flanking the foot of the drive provide eye-catching color most of the year and remain low enough so they won't block a driver's view. The foundation plantings contain compact plants that won't block the windows or the decorative wooden porch railing. The planting pocket marking the front walk holds low plants that won't engulf the lamppost or obscure light from the lamp.

The designer chose flagstones and cobblestones to complement the home's traditional clapboards. Flagstones in the walk and on the porch landing are mortared for weed-free upkeep, while the pavers leading around the garage are set in groundcover. The cobble inlay visually extends the plantings across the drive, and the edging serves as a mowing strip. The patches of lawn on both sides of the drive are designed for fast mowing. The ring of mulch under the tree protects the trunk and eliminates the need to hand trim.

Regionalized Plant Lists

Because climate and growing conditions vary greatly throughout North America, it is impossible to list here all the plants for this landscape plan that would do well everywhere on the continent. However, you can order a Blueprint Package with plant lists keyed to this plan and selected by expert horticulturists to thrive in your area.

The six-page Blueprint Package features a large-size version of this Plan View, plus a detailed regional Plant and Materials List. It also includes an illustrated list of hundreds of landscape plants suited to your region, in case you wish to make substitutions, as well as planting instructions and plant adaptation maps to ensure professional results with your new landscape.

See page 98 to order your regionalized Blueprint Package.

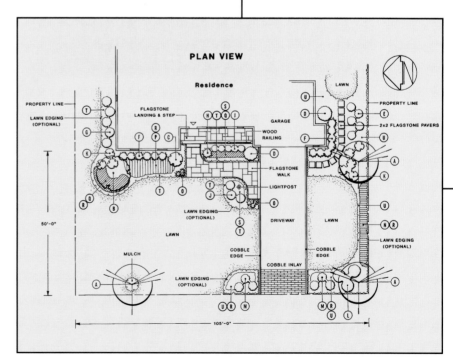

Landscape Plan L290 shown in spring

Designed by Jeffrey Diefenbach

Home Plan 2947
For information about ordering
blueprints for this home
call 1-800-521-6797.

This easy-care landscape contains graceful shade trees, compact shrubs, and an assortment of colorful perennials and bulbs. Weed-free flagstones and cobblestones complement the home's wood siding.

Rustic Tudor Home

The landscape around this rustic stone-fronted house is truly charming. The designer organizes the space into separate, easily maintained units that blend into a pleasing whole. The planting pockets—in front of the large window and the two areas bisected by pavers to the right of the drive—contain well-behaved plants that require little care to maintain their good looks. The small island of lawn can be quickly mowed, and maintenance is further reduced if lawn edging, which eliminates the need to edge by hand, is installed. A ribbon of small and moderate-sized shrubs, underplanted with a weed-smothering groundcover and spring bulbs, surrounds the lawn.

A single deciduous tree, set in a circle of bulbs and easy-care perennials that juts into the lawn, screens the entryway from street view and balances a triad of slow-growing, narrow conifers to the far left of the house. Shrubs in front of the windows were chosen for their low, unobtrusive growth habit. A dwarf conifer with pendulous branches forms the focus of the shrub grouping in front of the larger window.

Paving is a strong unifying force in this design. The stone in the house facade is echoed in the walk that curves from the driveway up the steps to the landing and front door. Flagstone pavers border the other side of the drive and lead around the house. The cobblestone inlay at the foot of the drive not only breaks up the monotony of the asphalt, but also visually carries the lawn border across the entire width of the property.

Landscape Plan L284 shown in spring

Designed by Salvatore A. Masullo

Regionalized Plant Lists

Because climate and growing conditions vary greatly throughout North America, it is impossible to list here all the plants that would do well everywhere on the continent. However, you can order a Blueprint Package for this plan containing a list of plants, selected by experts, for your region.

The six-page Blueprint Package features a large-size version of this Plan View, plus a detailed Plant and Materials List. It also includes an illustrated list of hundreds of landscape plants suited to your region, to use if you wish to make substitutions, as well as planting instructions and plant adaptation maps to ensure professional-looking results.

See page 98 to order your regionalized Blueprint Package.

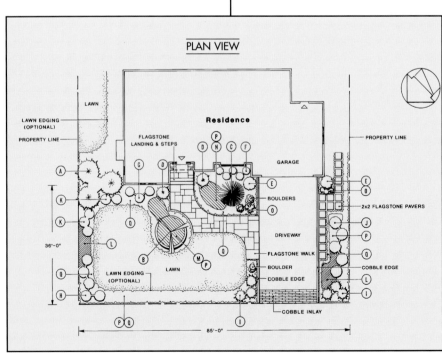

PLAN VIEW

Home Plan 2854
For information about ordering blueprints
for this home call 1-800-521-6797.

*Although packed with interesting plants, this landscape
is quite manageable for the easy-care gardener. Mowing
the little island of lawn is a snap, and caring for the
rest of the yard is just as easy, considering the shrubs
don't need pruning and fall cleanup is minimal.*

Williamsburg Cape

This extended Cape poses several challenges to the designer. Situated on a corner lot, the house needs access to both streets, but the noise from cars stopping at the intersection needs to be muffled. The two doors located in the front of the house should be distinguished and the long lines of the house played down. The landscape design provides walks leading to both entries while clearly defining the dominant, main entrance with a formal brick entry court. Partially hidden by an upright shrub, the entrance to the breezeway remains out of view but is still easily accessible by family members. The semicircular planting bed in front of the walkway leading to the breezeway breaks up the long lines of the brick walk and lawn while balancing the large planting beds beside the house.

The landscape on either side of the front door features symmetrically placed trees and shrubs to reflect the formality of the brick entryway. Tall, uniformly oval trees complement the formal design while softening the long lines of the house.

Because the house is located on a corner, access to the street with a front walkway is desirable. For unity and harmony, the same brick used in the walkway across the front of the house is used in the front walk. An extensive shrub border screens the view of the house from the intersection and stifles traffic noise. A variety of shrubs and perennials make up this border, to provide interest throughout the year.

Landscape Plan L201 shown in autumn

Designed by Michael J. Opisso

Regionalized Plant Lists

Because climate and growing conditions vary greatly throughout North America, it is impossible to list here all the plants that would do well everywhere on the continent. However, you can order a Blueprint Package for this plan containing a list of plants, selected by experts, for your region.

The six-page Blueprint Package features a large-size version of this Plan View, plus a detailed Plant and Materials List. It also includes an illustrated list of hundreds of landscape plants suited to your region, to use if you wish to make substitutions, as well as planting instructions and plant adaptation maps to ensure professional-looking results.

See page 98 to order your regionalized Blueprint Package.

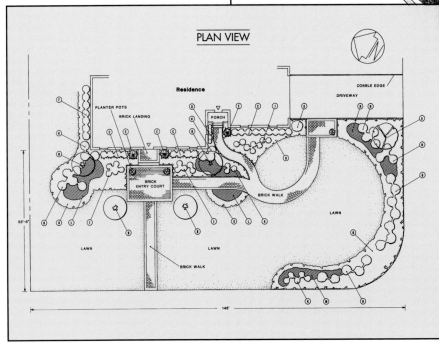

PLAN VIEW

Residence

PLANTER POTS

BRICK LANDING

PORCH

COBBLE EDGE

DRIVEWAY

BRICK ENTRY COURT

BRICK WALK

LAWN

LAWN

LAWN

BRICK WALK

53'-6"

146'

Home Plan 2520
For information about ordering blueprints for this home
call 1-800-521-6797.

Corner properties pose special landscaping challenges. Here the landscape designer screens the street with a colorful shrub border. A formal walkway leads from the main street, where guests might park, to the front door. A more informal walk provides access from the driveway to both entrances.

Folk Victorian Home

Graceful, curving foundation plantings really make this landscape! Set against a carpet of green grass, the mixed plantings contain shrubs, perennials, bulbs and groundcovers chosen for compactness as well as for attractive foliage and flowers. One of a trio of handsome multi-trunked deciduous trees with attractive peeling bark anchors the largest planting. Set near the porch, the tree contributes cool shade during the summer.

The tree to the far left softens the driveway, as do the cobblestones bordering the asphalt. Like the cobbles, the other paving materials—brick and flagstone—are selected for their compatibility with the house style. A brick walk leads to an arching entry landing set at the base of the stairs. The curved landing and planting beds echo the curves in the porch detail and some of the windows. Both the walk and terrace are edged with flagstone, a material repeated in the pavers leading from the opposite side of the driveway to the back of the house.

The third tree in the triangle is planted at the front of the lawn, where its picturesque bark can be admired close up by passersby. At the same time that the tree attracts attention, it also provides some screening and privacy. It is set in a ring of mulch for easy mowing.

Regionalized Plant Lists

Because climate and growing conditions vary greatly throughout North America, it is impossible to list here all the plants that would do well everywhere on the continent. However, you can order a Blueprint Package for this plan containing a list of plants, selected by experts, for your region.

The six-page Blueprint Package features a large-size version of this Plan View, plus a detailed Plant and Materials List. It also includes an illustrated list of hundreds of landscape plants suited to your region, to use if you wish to make substitutions, as well as planting instructions and plant adaptation maps to ensure professional-looking results.

See page 98 to order your regionalized Blueprint Package.

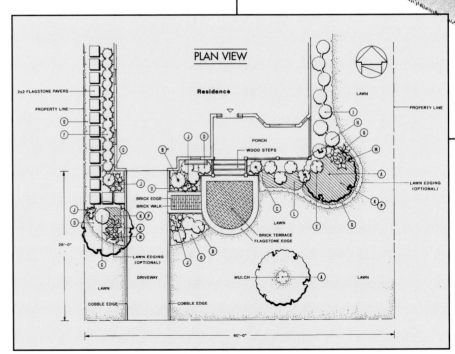

PLAN VIEW

Landscape Plan L283
shown in summer

Designed by Damon Scott

Home Plan 2974
For information about ordering blueprints
for this home call 1-800-521-6797.

*The foundation border curving around the house
provides the main source of interest in this landscape. However, maintaining it won't tax the
easy-care gardener because the plants are compact
and disease-resistant.*

**Landscape Plan L207
shown in summer**

Designed by David Poplaws

*Graceful trees, curving lines and bursts of flowers blooming
from spring through fall complement this comfortable country
retreat. The friendly landscaping creates the perfect finishing
touch that says: here's a place to hang up a hammock and relax.*

Country-Style Farmhouse

Set in a friendly and homey landscape brimming with flowers from spring through fall, this farmhouse's country atmosphere is now complete. Masses of perennials and bulbs used throughout the property create a garden setting and provide armloads of flowers that can be cut for indoor bouquets. But the floral beauty doesn't stop there; the designer artfully incorporates unusual specimens of summer- and fall-blooming trees and shrubs into the landscape design to elevate the changing floral scene to eye-level and above.

To match the informal mood of the house, both front walkway and driveway cut a curved, somewhat meandering path. A parking spur at the end of the driveway provides extra parking space and a place to turn around. Fieldstones, whose rustic character complements the country setting, pave the front walk. The stone piers and picket fence at the entrance to the driveway frame the entry and match the detail and character of the house's stone foundation and porch railing. The stone wall at the side of the property further carries out this theme.

Large specimen trees planted in the lawn set the house back from the road and provide a show of autumn color. Imagine completing the country theme in this tranquil setting by hanging a child's swing from the tree nearest the front porch.

Home Plan 2774

or information about ordering blueprints for this home call 1-800-521-6797.

Regionalized Plant Lists

Because climate and growing conditions vary greatly throughout North America, it is impossible to list here all the plants that would do well everywhere on the continent. However, you can order a Blueprint Package for this plan containing a list of plants, selected by experts, for your region.

The six-page Blueprint Package features a large-size version of this Plan View, plus a detailed Plant and Materials List. It also includes an illustrated list of hundreds of landscape plants suited to your region, to use if you wish to make substitutions, as well as planting instructions and plant adaptation maps to ensure professional-looking results.

See page 98 to order your regionalized Blueprint Package.

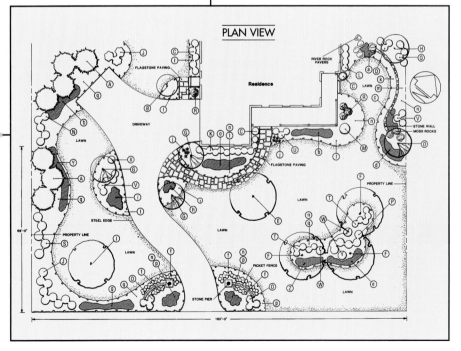

PLAN VIEW

Woodland Wildflower Walk

L arge trees create the woodland look of this plan, which provides exactly the right environment for the native shrubs and the delicate wildflowers and ferns that need a bit of shade to flourish. If you're lucky enough to have several large trees on site and perhaps are despairing over what to grow in their shade, this plan is your answer. If you have a sunny yard but yearn for shade, plant the largest slow-growing kinds of trees you can afford, balanced by a few fast-growing kinds. Plan on removing the faster, shorter-lived trees in a few years when the more desirable trees gain some stature. Ideal slow-growing trees to consider include native oaks and sugar maples. Fast growers that can be used to create shade and scale in a hurry include alders, poplars, and willows.

Wood-chip pathways throughout the mulched wildflower border make movement through the garden easy and inviting, creating vignettes at their corners and curves. The pond and the bridge that spans it anchor the design and lend the garden its unique character. Evergreen and deciduous trees and shrubs, including many natives, provide year-round structure.

At first, the wildflowers will grow in the spaces where you plant them, in exciting drifts of color. Over time, however, they'll mingle and reseed, creating a more natural unplanned look. Please be sure to purchase nursery-propagated wildflower plants and seeds; never transplant them from the wild or buy them from sources that gather them in the wild, since doing so further endangers the beauty of our natural heritage.

Regionalized Plant Lists

Because climate and growing conditions vary greatly throughout North America, it is impossible to list here all the plants that would do well everywhere on the continent. However, you can order a Blueprint Package for this plan containing a list of plants, selected by experts, for your region.

The six-page Blueprint Package features a large-size version of this Plan View, plus a detailed Plant and Materials List. It also includes an illustrated list of hundreds of landscape plants suited to your region, to use if you wish to make substitutions, as well as planting instructions and plant adaptation maps to ensure professional-looking results.

See page 98 to order your regionalized Blueprint Package.

Landscape Plan L260 shown in spring

Designed by Damon Scott and Jim Morgan

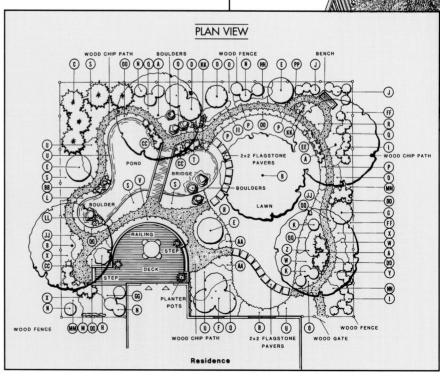

PLAN VIEW

WOOD CHIP PATH   BOULDERS   WOOD FENCE   BENCH

POND   BRIDGE   2x2 FLAGSTONE PAVERS   BOULDERS   LAWN   WOOD CHIP PATH

BOULDER   RAILING   STEP   DECK   STEP   PLANTER POTS

WOOD FENCE   WOOD CHIP PATH   2x2 FLAGSTONE PAVERS   WOOD GATE   WOOD FENCE

Residence

Admire your lovely woodland on a summer evening from the convenience of the raised deck, or at midday from the shaded, secluded bench in the far corner. Gentle curves, punctuated by wildflowers, boulders, and trees, invite a peaceful stroll through the woodland.

Naturalistic Grass Garden

Many cultures seem to have an identifiable garden style—there are formal Italian fountain gardens, French parterres, English perennial borders, and Japanese contemplation gardens. For many years, we didn't have an American-style garden. Now, a new trend has arisen, which the originators have dubbed the "New American Garden." This style of landscaping is naturalistic and relies on sweeps of ornamental grasses to create the feel of the prairies that once dominated much of the American landscape.

The backyard garden presented here follows that theme. The grasses used vary from low-growing plants hugging the borders to tall plants reaching 6 feet or more. Some of the grasses are bold and upright; others arching and graceful. When the grasses flower, they produce plumes that dance in the wind and sparkle in the sun. Foliage colors include bright green, blue-green, variegated, and even blood-red. During autumn, foliage and flowers dry in place, forming a stunning scene of naturalistic hues in varying shades of straw, almond, brown, and rust. Most of the grasses remain interesting to look at all winter, unless heavy snow flattens them to the ground. In early spring, the dried foliage must be cut off and removed to make way for new growth—but this is the only maintenance chore required by an established garden of ornamental grasses!

The design includes a large realistic-looking pond, which can be made from a vinyl-liner or concrete. At the end of the path leading from the bridge, a small seating area provides a retreat.

Landscape Plan L246 shown in summer

Designed by Damon Scott

Regionalized Plant Lists

Because climate and growing conditions vary greatly throughout North America, it is impossible to list here all the plants that would do well everywhere on the continent. However, you can order a Blueprint Package for this plan containing a list of plants, selected by experts, for your region.

The six-page Blueprint Package features a large-size version of this Plan View, plus a detailed Plant and Materials List. It also includes an illustrated list of hundreds of landscape plants suited to your region, to use if you wish to make substitutions, as well as planting instructions and plant adaptation maps to ensure professional-looking results.

See page 98 to order your regionalized Blueprint Package.

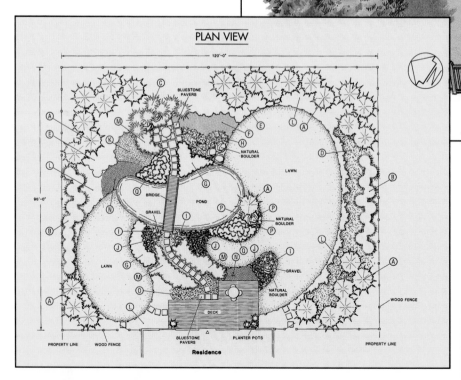

PLAN VIEW

Low in maintenance requirements, high in natural appeal, this garden of ornamental grasses delights the senses all year with subdued foliage colors, sparkling flower plumes, and rustling leaves.

Landscape Plan L253 shown in summer

Designed by Michael J. Opisso
and Damon Scott

This backyard features not one, but two, ponds in which to dip your toes during summer's heat. If you choose to keep your shoes on, sit on the patio near the large pond or on the bench by the small one to cool off in the reflection of the colorful surroundings.

Water Garden

There are few places more tranquil, more relaxing, or more cooling on a hot summer day than a garden with a view of the water—even if the water is no more than a garden pool. In the garden pictured here, two ponds filled with water lilies are used to create a tranquil setting. The first pond is situated near the house, where it is visible from the indoors. The deck is cantilevered over the pond to enhance the closeness of the water, and is covered with an overhead trellis, which ties the two areas together. The trellising also frames the view of the pond from the deck, and of the deck from the garden areas.

A second, smaller pond is set into the corner of the garden and has a backdrop of early-spring flowering trees, ferns, and shade-loving perennials. This intimate retreat is made complete by setting a bench and planter pots beside the pond.

Throughout the property, river-rock paving enhances the natural feeling of the water and provides a sitting area nearby for quiet contemplation. Moss rocks, placed in strategic places in the garden, further carry out the naturalistic theme, as do most of the landscape plants. The shrubs and perennials bordering the undulating lawn provide the needed soft-textured, informal look that makes both ponds seem natural and right at home.

Regionalized Plant Lists

Because climate and growing conditions vary greatly throughout North America, it is impossible to list here all the plants that would do well everywhere on the continent. However, you can order a Blueprint Package for this plan containing a list of plants, selected by experts, for your region.

The six-page Blueprint Package features a large-size version of this Plan View, plus a detailed Plant and Materials List. It also includes an illustrated list of hundreds of landscape plants suited to your region, to use if you wish to make substitutions, as well as planting instructions and plant adaptation maps to ensure professional-looking results.

See page 98 to order your regionalized Blueprint Package.

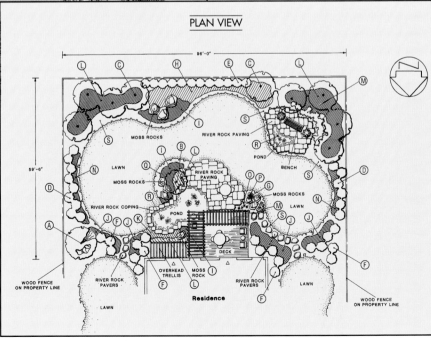

PLAN VIEW

Garden to Attract Birds

There is no better way to wake up in the morning than to the sound of songbirds in the garden. Wherever you live, you will be surprised at the number and variety of birds you can attract by offering them a few basic necessities—water, shelter, nesting spots, and food. Birds need water for drinking and bathing. They need shrubs and trees, especially evergreens, for shelter and nesting. Edge spaces—open areas with trees nearby for quick protection—provide ground feeders with foraging places, while plants with berries and nuts offer other natural sources of food.

The garden presented here contains all the necessary elements to attract birds to the garden. The shrubs and trees are chosen especially to provide a mix of evergreen and deciduous species. All of these, together with the masses of flowering perennials, bear seeds, nuts or berries are known to appeal to birds. The berry show looks quite pretty, too, until the birds gobble them up. Planted densely enough for necessary shelter, the bird-attracting plants create a backyard that's enjoyable throughout the seasons.

The birdbath is located in the lawn so it will be in the sun. A naturalistic pond provides water in a more protected setting. The birdhouses and feeders aren't necessary—though they may be the icing on the cake when it comes to luring the largest number of birds—because the landscape provides abundant natural food and shelter. Outside one of the main windows of the house, a birdfeeder hangs from a small flowering tree, providing up-close viewing of your feathered friends.

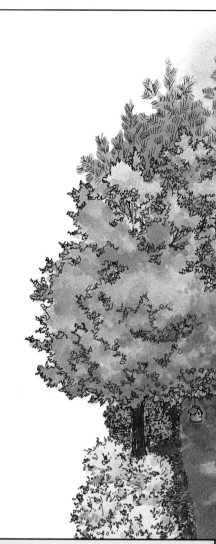

Regionalized Plant Lists

Because climate and growing conditions vary greatly throughout North America, it is impossible to list here all the plants that would do well everywhere on the continent. However, you can order a Blueprint Package for this plan containing a list of plants, selected by experts, for your region.

The six-page Blueprint Package features a large-size version of this Plan View, plus a detailed Plant and Materials List. It also includes an illustrated list of hundreds of landscape plants suited to your region, to use if you wish to make substitutions, as well as planting instructions and plant adaptation maps to ensure professional-looking results.

See page 98 to order your regionalized Blueprint Package.

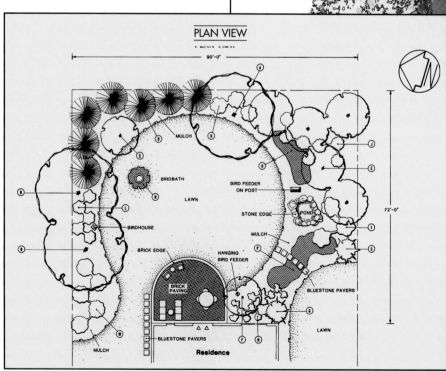

PLAN VIEW

Landscape Plan L245
shown in autumn
Designed by
Michael J. Opisso

Nature lovers will delight in the abundant birds that will flock to this beautiful garden. An attractive collection of berried plants and evergreens offers food and shelter for the wildlife, while creating a handsome, pastoral setting.

Landscape Plan L252 shown in summer

Designed by Michael J. Opisso

A cook's garden, this backyard provides everything the family needs to eat. The vegetable garden is integrated into the yard in a manner more attractive than usual vegetable gardens, and the shrub borders feature berry plants and fruit trees.

Edible Landscape

The suburban food gardener needn't worry about turning the backyard into unattractive rows of vegetables when following this innovative design. Here is a backyard that looks good enough to eat! It is designed to produce abundant, fresh, home-grown produce and still be a beautiful spot for relaxing and entertaining. Though the main feature of the property is a central vegetable garden, many of the landscape plants used in the border plantings and along the house produce edible fruit as well. These plants were especially chosen because they can perform double duty, acting both as ornamentals and as food-producers.

The vegetable garden is accessible by way of a short path around the lawn. The garden is designed in a round form for greater interest, and has gravel paths dissecting it for ease of working and harvesting. Even in winter, when bare of plantings, this garden will be attractive to look at because of its geometrical layout. The designer has left the choice of vegetables up to the gardener and chef, but there is plenty of space to grow the family's favorite choices. Off to the side, a storage shed provides needed space for storing wheelbarrow, hoe, and other gardening paraphernalia. A compost pile is conveniently located out of sight behind the shed.

The outdoor kitchen area on the brick patio contains a barbecue, a sink, and a serving cabinet that doubles as a bar. Covered with an overhead lattice to set off the chef's culinary preparation area, this part of the patio provides a comfortable spot in which to lounge and dine out of the sun. For sunning, move out from under the lattice and soak up the rays.

Regionalized Plant Lists

Because climate and growing conditions vary greatly throughout North America, it is impossible to list here all the plants that would do well everywhere on the continent. However, you can order a Blueprint Package for this plan containing a list of plants, selected by experts, for your region.

The six-page Blueprint Package features a large-size version of this Plan View, plus a detailed Plant and Materials List. It also includes an illustrated list of hundreds of landscape plants suited to your region, to use if you wish to make substitutions, as well as planting instructions and plant adaptation maps to ensure professional-looking results.

See page 98 to order your regionalized Blueprint Package.

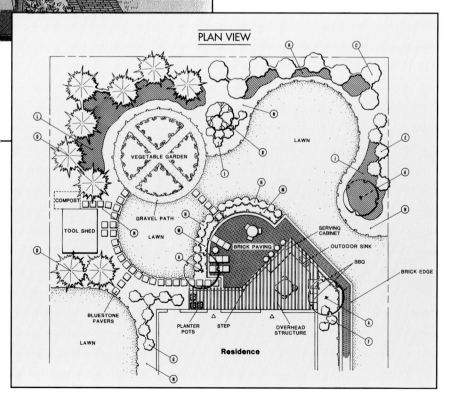

PLAN VIEW

VEGETABLE GARDEN
LAWN
COMPOST
GRAVEL PATH
TOOL SHED
LAWN
SERVING CABINET
BRICK PAVING
OUTDOOR SINK
BBQ
BRICK EDGE
BLUESTONE PAVERS
LAWN
PLANTER POTS
STEP
OVERHEAD STRUCTURE
Residence

Landscape Plan L305
shown in summer

Designed by Michael J. Opisso

You'll spend many more hours just relaxing in this backyard retreat than you will taking care of it. Since there's no lawn, you'll escape weekly lawn mowing, and will even be able to leave the garden untended during extended vacations.

Effortless Informality

Your cares melt away when you enter this very private and tranquil garden through the vine-covered arbor. The designer sites an informal flagstone terrace with two seating areas in a sea of evergreen groundcover, entirely eliminating a lawn and making the garden about as carefree as it can be. Evergreens on the property border create privacy, while airy trees—selected because they cast light shade and are easy to clean up after—create a lacy overhead canopy. The overall effect is serene.

A half-circle rock wall, built of small, moss-covered boulders, sets off the larger of the two seating areas and gives dimension to the area. (Five moss rocks on the opposite side of the patio echo and balance the wall.) Several types of perennials spill over the top and sprout from the crevices of the wall, decorating the area with their dainty flowers and foliage and creating a soft, natural look. Large drifts of spring bulbs and other perennials make lovely splashes of color where they grow through the groundcover. Flowering shrubs—many of which also display evergreen leaves—give the garden year-round structure and interest, while offering easy-care floral beauty.

The lack of a lawn makes this garden especially easy to care for. The groundcover absorbs most of the leaves that drop from the deciduous trees in autumn, and the terrace can be quickly swept or blown free of leaves and debris, as needed. All you'll need to do is cut off the dead tops of the perennials once a year in late winter.

PLAN VIEW

PROPERTY LINE

PROPERTY LINE

34'-0"

MOSS ROCK
RETAINING WALL

PROPERTY LINE

FENCE

FLAGSTONE WALK
& TERRACE

MOSS ROCKS

ARBOR WITH GATE

FENCE

FLAGSTONE LANDING
& STEP WITH STONE RISER

Residence

60'-0"

Regionalized Plant Lists

Because climate and growing conditions vary greatly throughout North America, it is impossible to list here all the plants that would do well everywhere on the continent. However, you can order a Blueprint Package for this plan containing a list of plants, selected by experts, for your region.

The six-page Blueprint Package features a large-size version of this Plan View, plus a detailed Plant and Materials List. It also includes an illustrated list of hundreds of landscape plants suited to your region, to use if you wish to make substitutions, as well as planting instructions and plant adaptation maps to ensure professional-looking results.

See page 98 to order your regionalized Blueprint Package.

Dry Streambed

nspired by contemplative Oriental gardens, this naturalistic garden relies on boulders, a layer of gravel and a slope of fieldstone to suggest the bed of a former stream. A simple wooden footbridge leads over the stream to a gazebo at the right edge of the bed. The design includes a lovely palette of shrubs, perennials, small trees and ornamental grasses, all of which require minimal watering and, as an added bonus, are low-maintenance. This leaves you more time to spend in the gazebo meditating and contemplating your surroundings.

The bed, which can be located in any open area of your property, is dug to a depth of six feet. A layer of gravel lines the interior of the bed, giving it a natural appearance. The designer creates a berm on the upper side of the bed from the excavated soil. You may prefer to create a flatter design, digging instead to a depth of only one or two feet. Even this slight change in elevation is enough to create the desired effect of allowing the water-thrifty plants to flow over the banks and make a visual reference to a stream that is no longer there.

Regionalized Plant Lists

Because climate and growing conditions vary greatly throughout North America, it is impossible to list here all the plants that would do well everywhere on the continent. However, you can order a Blueprint Package for this plan containing a list of plants, selected by experts, for your region.

The six-page Blueprint Package features a large-size version of this Plan View, plus a detailed Plant and Materials List. It also includes an illustrated list of hundreds of landscape plants suited to your region, to use if you wish to make substitutions, as well as planting instructions and plant adaptation maps to ensure professional-looking results.

See page 98 to order your regionalized Blueprint Package.

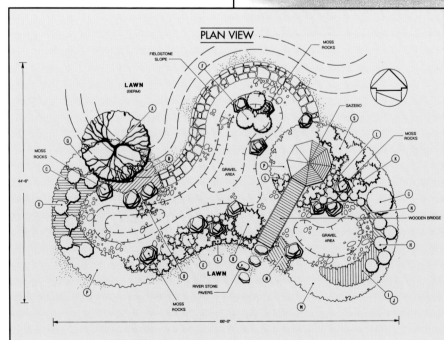

PLAN VIEW

Landscape Plan L316
shown in summer

Designed by Michael J. Opisso

*Pretty to look at, and easy to care for, this garden
features a rocky former streambed to complement
the drought-tolerant plants*

Old-Fashioned Roses and Perennials

A romantic old-fashioned rose border is always in style. The voluptuous fragrance and heavy-petaled blossoms of roses bring charm to any sunny garden. Here, the designer chooses old garden roses, which offer scent as well as ease of care, unlike modern hybrid tea roses. Although many of these cherished plants bloom only once during the season, their other charms far outweigh the repeat-blossoms of their modern cousins. Many have excellent summer and fall foliage and a heavy crop of glossy rose hips in autumn.

In this border design, these belles of the garden are mixed with classic perennial partners and bulbs to create months of color and interest. A circular bed is tucked into this pleasingly curved border and is separated by a ribbon-like strip of lawn. A rose-covered pergola in the border frames a classically inspired sculpture in the bed's center, creating two balanced focal points. A stone bench placed under the arbor provides a lovely spot to contemplate the wonders of this flower-filled haven. Mulched pathways at the back of the border allow easy access for maintenance and for cutting flowers for the house.

Landscape Plan L319 shown in summer

Designed by Maria Morrison

Regionalized Plant Lists

Because climate and growing conditions vary greatly throughout North America, it is impossible to list here all the plants that would do well everywhere on the continent. However, you can order a Blueprint Package for this plan containing a list of plants, selected by experts, for your region.

The six-page Blueprint Package features a large-size version of this Plan View, plus a detailed Plant and Materials List. It also includes an illustrated list of hundreds of landscape plants suited to your region, to use if you wish to make substitutions, as well as planting instructions and plant adaptation maps to ensure professional-looking results.

See page 98 to order your regionalized Blueprint Package.

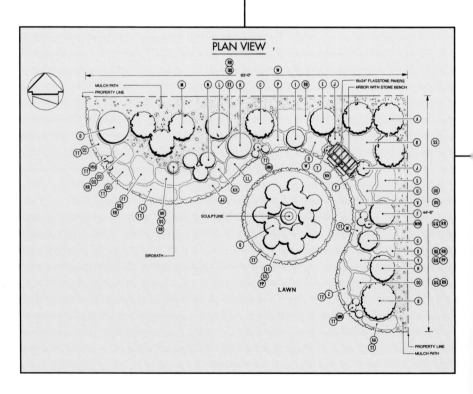

PLAN VIEW

Designed to beautify the corner of a backyard, this rose-filled border can be easily turned into a free-standing bed and placed in the center of a lawn by rounding off the straight sides into a more free-flowing shape.

Easy-Care Shrub Border

Nothing beats flowering shrubs and trees for an easy-care show of flowers and foliage throughout the seasons. This lovely garden includes shrubs that bloom at various times of the year—from late winter right into autumn—so that blossoms will always be decorating this garden. In autumn, the leaves of the deciduous shrubs turn flaming shades of yellow, gold, orange, and red. (These colors appear even more brilliant when juxtaposed against the deep greens of the evergreen shrubs.) During the coldest months, when the flowers and fall foliage are finally finished, many of the plants feature glossy red berries or evergreen leaves that take on deep burgundy hues.

The designer balanced the border with a tall evergreen and two flowering trees, which serve as anchors at the borders' widest points. Most shrubs are grouped in all-of-a-kind drifts to create the most impact—low, spreading types in the front and taller ones in the back—but several specimens appear alone as eye-catching focal points. A few large drifts of easy-care, long-blooming perennials, interplanted with spring-flowering bulbs, break up the shrubbery to give a variety of textures and forms.

Designed for the back of an average-sized lot, this easy-care border can be located in any sunny area of your property. It makes a perfect addition to any existing property with only a high-maintenance lawn and little other landscaping. The design adds year-round interest, creates privacy, and reduces maintenance.

Regionalized Plant Lists

Because climate and growing conditions vary greatly throughout North America, it is impossible to list here all the plants that would do well everywhere on the continent. However, you can order a Blueprint Package for this plan containing a list of plants, selected by experts, for your region.

The six-page Blueprint Package features a large-size version of this Plan View, plus a detailed Plant and Materials List. It also includes an illustrated list of hundreds of landscape plants suited to your region, to use if you wish to make substitutions, as well as planting instructions and plant adaptation maps to ensure professional-looking results.

See page 98 to order your regionalized Blueprint Package.

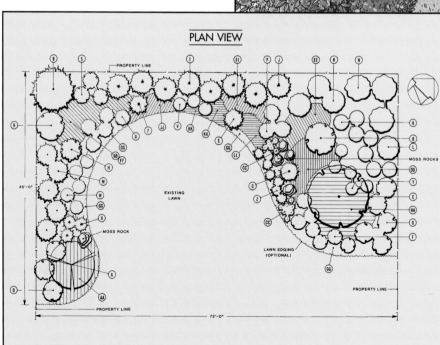

PLAN VIEW

Landscape Plan L308 shown in spring

Designed by Salvatore A. Masullo

When easy-care, disease- and insect-resistant shrubs are used to create a border, and allowed to grow naturally without excessive pruning, the result is a beautiful, practically maintenance-free garden.

Landscape Plan L276 shown in summer

Designed by Michael J. Opisso

The English perennial border with its graceful masses of ever-changing flowers represents the epitome of fine perennial gardening. Planted in a corner of your property, this garden will provide enjoyment for years to come.

English Perennial Border

The British, being renowned gardeners, boast the prettiest flower gardens in the world. Just the words *English perennial border* evoke instant images of masses of billowing blossoms, elegant hedges, and vine-draped thatched cottages. Their success in growing perennials to such perfection lies partly in the amenable British climate—cool summers, mild winters, plenty of moisture throughout the year, and very long summer days. Even without such a perfect climate, North American gardeners can achieve a respectable show of perennials by using plants better adapted to their climate. Arrange them into the flowing drifts made popular early in this century by British landscape designers, and you'll have the epitome of a perennial garden in your own backyard.

The perennial border shown here fits nicely into a corner of almost any sunny backyard. Pictured with a traditional evergreen hedge as a backdrop for the flowers, the garden looks equally lovely planted in front of a fence or house wall, as long as the area receives at least six hours of full sun a day.

The designer carefully selected an array of spring-, summer-, and fall-blooming perennials, arranging them in artful drifts for an ever-changing display. Spring and summer blooms paint a delightful pink, magenta, and pale yellow color scheme sparked here and there with splashes of white and blue, while autumn brings deeper colors—gold, dark pink, and purple. Patches of burgundy- and silver-hued foliage plants in the foreground help tie the elements of the garden together and play up the flowers.

Regionalized Plant Lists

Because climate and growing conditions vary greatly throughout North America, it is impossible to list here all the plants that would do well everywhere on the continent. However, you can order a Blueprint Package for this plan containing a list of plants, selected by experts, for your region.

The six-page Blueprint Package features a large-size version of this Plan View, plus a detailed Plant and Materials List. It also includes an illustrated list of hundreds of landscape plants suited to your region, to use if you wish to make substitutions, as well as planting instructions and plant adaptation maps to ensure professional-looking results.

See page 98 to order your regionalized Blueprint Package.

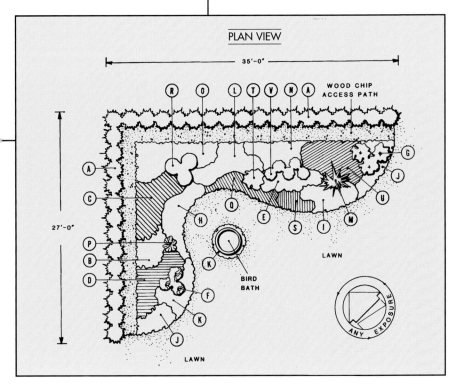

PLAN VIEW

35'-0"

WOOD CHIP ACCESS PATH

27'-0"

LAWN

BIRD BATH

ANY EXPOSURE

LAWN

ORDERING LANDSCAPE PLANS

The Landscape Plan Blueprint Package

The Landscape Blueprint Package available from Home Planners includes all the necessary information you need to lay out and install the landscape design of your choice. Professionally designed and prepared with attention to detail, these clear, easy-to-follow plans offer everything from a precise plot plan and regionalized plant and materials list to helpful sheets on installing your landscape and determining the mature size of your plants. These plans will help you achieve professional-looking results, adding value and enjoyment to your property for years to come.

Each set of blueprints is a full 18" x 24" in size with clear, complete instructions and easy-to-read type.

Consisting of six detailed sheets, these plans show how all plants and materials are put together to form an exciting landscape for your home.

To order your plans, simply find the Plan Number of the design of your choice in the Plans Index below. Consult the appropriate Price Schedule to determine the price of your plans, choosing the 1-, 3-, or 6-set package for Landscape Plans and any additional or reverse sets you desire. Make sure your Plant and Materials List contains the best selection for your area by referring to the Regional Order Map below and specifying the region in which you reside. Fill out the Order Coupon on the opposite page and mail it to us for prompt fulfillment or call our Toll-Free Order Hotline for even faster service.

Landscape Plans Price Schedule & Index

Landscape Plans	Page	Price	Available For Regions:
L201	72	Y	1-3, 5, 6 & 8
L207	76	Z	1-6, 8
L245	84	Y	ALL
L246	80	Z	ALL
L252	86	Y	ALL
L253	82	Z	ALL
L260	78	Z	1-3, 5, 6 & 8
L276	96	W	ALL
L283	74	X	ALL
L284	70	Y	ALL
L290	68	Y	ALL
L305	88	Y	ALL
L308	94	X	ALL
L316	90	Y	ALL
L319	92	Y	1-3, 5-8

Landscape Plans Price Schedule

Price Group	W	X	Y	Z
1 set	$25	$35	$45	$55
3 sets	$40	$50	$60	$70
6 sets	$55	$65	$75	$85
Additional Identical Sets . . . .$10 each				
Reverse Sets (Mirror Image) . . . . . .$10 each				

Specify the region in which you reside to make sure your Landscape Plant and Materials List contains the best selection for your area.

Regional Order Map

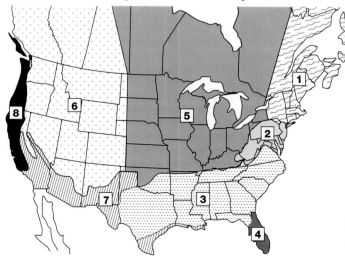

Region 1 Northeast
Region 2 Mid-Atlantic
Region 3 Deep South
Region 4 Florida & Gulf Coast
Region 5 Midwest
Region 6 Rocky Mountains
Region 7 Southern California
             & Desert Southwest
Region 8 Northern California
             & Pacific Northwest

TO ORDER: Just clip the accompanying order blank and mail with your check or money order. If you prefer, you can also use a credit card. If time is of essence, call us Toll-Free at 1-800-521-6797 on our Blueprint Hotline. We try to process and ship every order within 48 hours. Because of this quick turnaround, we won't send a formal notice acknowledging receipt of your order. If you use the coupon, please include the correct postage and handling charges.

OUR EXCHANGE POLICY

Because we produce and ship plans in response to individual orders, we cannot honor requests for refunds. However, you can exchange your entire order of blueprints, including a single set if you order just one, for a set of another design. All exchanges carry an additional fee of $15.00 plus $15.00 for postage and handling if they're sent via surface mail; $20.00 for priority air mail and $30 via express.

ABOUT REVERSE BLUEPRINTS

If you want to install your landscape in reverse of the plan as shown, we will include an extra set of blueprints with the Frontal Sheet and Plan View reversed for an additional fee of $10.00. Although callouts and lettering appear backward, reverses will prove useful as a visual aid if you decide to flop the plan.

HOW MANY BLUEPRINTS DO YOU NEED
FOR LANDSCAPE PLANS?

To study your favorite landscape design or make alterations of the plan to fit your site, one set of blueprints may be sufficient. On the other hand, if you plan to install the landscape yourself using subcontractors or have a general contractor do the work for you, you will probably need more sets. Because you save money on 3-set or 6-set packages, you should consider ordering all the sets at one time.

FOR CUSTOMER SERVICE
CALL TOLL FREE
1-888-690-1116

BLUEPRINT HOTLINE
CALL TOLL FREE 1-800-521-6797. We try to process and ship every order within two business days. When you order by phone, please be prepared to give us the Order Form Key Number shown in the box at the bottom of the Order Form.

By FAX: Copy the order form at right and send on our FAX line: 1-800-224-6699 or 1-520-544-3086.

CANADIAN CUSTOMERS

ORDER TOLL FREE 1-800-561-4169
For faster service and plans that are modified for building in Canada, customers may now call in orders directly to our Canadian supplier of plans and charge the purchase to a charge card. Or, you may complete the order form at right, adding 40% to all prices and mail in Canadian funds to:

> THE PLAN CENTRE
> 60 Baffin Place
> Unit 5
> Waterloo, Ontario N2V 1Z7

By FAX: Copy the Order Form at right and send it via our Canadian FAX line: 1-800-719-3291.

BLUEPRINTS ARE
NOT RETURNABLE

BLUEPRINT ORDER FORM

HOME PLANNERS, LLC
Wholly owned by Hanley-Wood, Inc.
3275 WEST INA ROAD, SUITE 110
TUCSON, ARIZONA 85741

Please rush me the following:
_____ Set(s) of Landscape Plan _____
     (See Index and Price Schedule) $ _____
_____ Additional identical blueprints in
     same order at $10 per set. $ _____
_____ Reverse blueprints at $10 per set. $ _____

Please indicate the appropriate region of the country for Plant and Materials List (see map on opposite page):
- ☐ Region 1   Northeast
- ☐ Region 2   Mid-Atlantic
- ☐ Region 3   Deep South
- ☐ Region 4   Florida & Gulf Coast
- ☐ Region 5   Midwest
- ☐ Region 6   Rocky Mountains
- ☐ Region 7   Southern California & Desert Southwest
- ☐ Region 8   Northern California & Pacific Northwest

POSTAGE AND HANDLING		
Carrier Delivery (Requires street address—No P.O Boxes)		
• Regular Service (Allow 7-10 days delivery)	$8.00	$ _____
• Priority (Allow 4-5 days delivery)	$12.00	$ _____
• Express (Allow 3 days delivery)	$22.00	$ _____
Certified Mail (requires signature) If no street address available. (Allow 7-10 days delivery)	$12.00	$ _____
Overseas Delivery	Phone, FAX or Mail for Quote	

NOTE: All delivery times are from date blueprint package is shipped.

POSTAGE (from box above) $ _____
SUB-TOTAL $ _____
SALES TAX (AZ, MI, & WA residents,
      please add appropriate state and local tax.) $ _____
TOTAL (Sub-Total and Tax) $ _____

YOUR ADDRESS (please print)
Name _____
Street_____
City _____ State _____ ZIP _____
Daytime telephone number (_____) _____

FOR CREDIT CARD ORDERS ONLY
Please fill in the information below:

Credit card number _____
Exp. Date: Month/Year _____
Check One: ☐ Visa   ☐ MasterCard   ☐ Discover Card
Signature _____

ORDER TOLL FREE
1-800-521-6797 or
1-520-297-8200

Order Form Key
TB60

Company Index

The 3E Group
P.O. Box 392
Moorestown, NJ 08057
609-866-7600
1-800-800-2844
Fax: 609-866-7603

A-1 Unique Insect Control
5504 Sperry Dr.
Citrus Heights, CA 95621
916-961-7945
Fax: 916-967-7082
www.a-1unique.com

AAA Aluminum Products
1710 Gilmore Ave.
Burnaby, BC V5C 4T3
Canada
604-298-7241

AB Cushing Mills
7103 - 30 St., S.E.
Box 39, Station T
Calgary, AB T2H 2G7
Canada
403-279-8800
Fax: 403-279-0077

Abatron
5501 95th Ave.
Kenosha, WI 53144
414-653-2000
1-800-445-1754
Fax: 414-653-2019
www.abatron.com

Abrasive Systems
6130 Old Jonestown Rd.
Harrisburg, PA 17112
717-540-6868
1-800-288-7800
Fax: 717-540-6871

Abundant Energy
P.O. Box 307
Pine Island, NY 10969
914-258-4022
1-800-426-4859

Abundant Life Seed Foundation
P.O. Box 772
Port Townsend, WA 98368
360-385-5660
Fax: 360-385-7455
csf.colorado.edu/
perma/abundant

Ace Hardware Corp.
2200 Kensington Ct.

Oak Brook, IL 60521
630-990-1240
Fax: 630-990-9707

Adventures in Herbs
P.O. Box 23240
Mint Hill, NC 28227
704-882-2669
Only in South

agAccess Book Catalog
P.O. Box 2008
Davis, CA 95617
530-756-7177
1-800-540-0170
Fax: 530-756-7188
www.agribooks.com

Age-Old Organics
P.O. Box 618,
2001 N. Main St.
Mendota, IL 61342
1-800-255-4906
Fax: 815-538-6981
www.fertiler.grower.com

Air Aqua Enterprises
3210 W. Lake Ave.
Glenview, IL 60025-1209
847-657-9655
1-800-454-1631
Fax: 847-657-9658

Air Expose
4703 Leffingwell St.
Houston, TX 77026-3434
713-672-7017

Akzo Nobel Coatings
P.O. Box 7062,
1845 Maxwell
Troy, MI 48007
810-637-0400
1-800-833-7288 (US)
1-800-663-6273 (Canada)
Fax: 810-649-6529

Aldon Corp.
6426 Hwy. 93 S.
Whitefish, MT 59937
406-862-6050
Fax: 800-332-9329
www.aldonchem.com

Alko-America
801 E. Morehead St.,
Ste. 303
Charlotte, NC 28202-2729
704-343-0430
Fax: 704-343-0430
E-mail:geodill@aol.com

Allen Plant Co.
P.O. Box 310
Fruitland, MD
21826-0310
410-742-7122
Fax: 410-742-7120
www.imox.com/allenplant

Almost Heaven
Rt. 5 HP
Renick, WV 24966
304-497-3163
Fax: 304-497-2698
www.almostheaven.net

Alpine Gardens
12446 County F
Stitzer, WI 53825

Alsto's Handy Helpers
P.O. Box 1267
Galesburg, IL 61402-1267
309-343-6181
1-800-447-0048
Fax: 800-522-5786

ALUMET Building Products
227 Town East Blvd.
P.O. Box 850163
Mesquite, TX 75185-0163
214-285-8811
1-800-827-6045
Fax: 214-882-8813

Amdega Machin Conservatories
P.O. Box 7
Glenview, IL 60025
1-800-922-0110

American Arborist Supplies
882 S. Matlack St.
West Chester, PA
19382-4502
610-430-1214
1-800-441-8381
Fax: 610-430-8560
www.arborist.com

The American Botanist, Booksellers
P.O. Box 532,
1103 W. Truitt Ave.
Chillicothe, IL 61523
309-274-5254
Fax: 309-274-6143
E-mail:agbook@mtco.com

American ConForm Industries
1820 S. Santa Fe
Santa Ana, CA 92705
714-662-1100
1-800-CONFORM
Fax: 714-662-0405

American Lantern Div.
Inteletron
21021 Corsair Blvd.
Hayward, CA 94545
510-732-6790
1-800-556-2387
Fax: 510-732-6910

American Lawn Mower Co./Great States Corp.
P.O. Box 369
Shelbyville, IN 46176
317-392-3615
1-800-633-1501
Fax: 317-392-4118
www.reelin.com

American Lighting
5211D W. Market St.
Ste. 803
Greensboro, NC 27265
1-800-741-0571

American Lighting Assn.
World Trade Center
P.O. Box 420288
Dallas, TX 75342-0288
214-698-9898
1-800-605-4448
Fax: 214-698-9899

American Plant Products & Service
9200 N.W. 10th St.
Oklahoma City, OK
73127-7430
405-787-4833
1-800-522-3376
Fax: 405-789-2352
www.americanplant.com

American Polysteel Forms
5150 F Edith, N.E.
Albuquerque, NM 87107
505-345-8153
1-800-977-3676
Fax: 505-345-8154
www.polysteel.com

American Site Furniture
P.O. Box 158
56 Winthrop St.
Concord, MA 01742
508-371-3080
1-800-366-3080
Fax: 508-369-4472

American Standard Co./Florian® Ratchet-Cut®
157 Water St.
Southington, CT 06489
860-628-9643
1-800-275-3618
Fax: 860-628-6036
www.florianratchetcut.com

American Stone-Mix
8320 Bellona Ave.
Towson, MD 21204-2086
410-296-6770
1-800-445-8250
Fax: 410-494-0897
www.amspec.com

American Technocrete Corp.
3518 Cahuenga Blvd. W.
Ste. 200
Los Angeles, CA 90068
213-874-2427
1-800-624-9255
Fax: 213-874-4338

American Willow Growers Network
412 County Rd. 31
Norwich, NY 13815-3149
607-336-9031
Fax: 607-336-9031
www.msu.edu/user/shermanh/galeb/

Americana Bldg. Products By Hindman Manufacturing
P.O. Box 1290
Salem, IL 62881
618-548-2800
1-800-851-0865
Fax: 618-548-2890
www.americana.com

Amerigrow Recycling
10320 W. Atlantic Ave.
Delray Beach, FL 33446-9752
561-499-8148
Fax: 561-499-5896
E-mail:amergrow@bellsouth.net
Only in South

Ampro Industries
P.O. Box 6
Bradley, MI 49311-0006
616-792-2241
1-800-632-1998
Fax: 616-792-1700
www.amturf.com

Anchor Decking Systems
518 N.W. 77th St.
Boca Raton, FL 33483
561-982-9966
1-888-898-4990
Fax: 561-241-4591
E-mail:topdeck007@aol.com

Anchor Wall Systems
6101 Baker Rd., Ste. 201
Minnetonka, MN 55345-5973
612-933-8855
1-800-473-4452
Fax: 612-933-8833
www.anchorwall.com

Anderson Design/Garden Arches
P.O. Box 4057-H
Bellingham, WA 98227
360-650-1587
Fax: 360-650-0733
www.gardenarches.com

Ann Mann's Orchids
9045 Ron-Den Ln.
Windemere, FL 34786
407-876-2625
www.cfog.com

Appalachian Gardens
P.O. Box 82
Waynesboro, PA 17268
717-762-4312
Fax: 717-762-7532
E-mail:appgarden@innernet.net

Aqua Plunge
Aqua Plunge Div.
6101 49th St. S.
Muscatine, IA 52761
319-263-6642
1-800-553-9664
Fax: 319-263-8358

Aquatic Industries
P.O. Box 889
Leander, TX 78646-0889
512-259-2255
Fax: 512-259-3633

Arbor Systems LLC
10168 L St.
Omaha, NE 68127-1120
402-339-4459
1-800-698-4641

Fax: 402-339-5011
www.arborsystemsllc.com

Architectural Landscape Lighting
2930 S. Fairview St.
Santa Ana, CA 92704
1-800-854-8277
Fax: 714-668-1107
E-mail:alllighting@earthlink.com

Ardee Lighting
P.O. Box 1769
Shelby, NC 28151
704-482-2811
1-800-275-1544

Ardisam
1360 1st Ave.
Cumberland, WI 54829
715-822-2415
1-800-345-6007
Fax: 715-822-4180

Argee Corp.
9550 Pathway St.
Santee, CA 92071-4169
619-449-5050
Fax: 619-449-8392

Aristech Acrylics
7350 Empire Dr.
Florence, KY 41042
606-283-1501
1-800-354-9858
Fax: 606-283-7377
www.thedreamhome.com

Arriscraft Intl.
875 Speedsville Rd.
P.O. Box 3190
Cambridge, ON N3H 4S8
Canada
519-653-3275
1-800-265-8123
Fax: 519-653-1337
www.arriscraft.com

Artistic Enclosures
5 Willow St. Industrial Pk.
Fleetwood, PA 19522
610-944-8585
1-800-944-8599
Fax: 610-944-8120
Only in Midwest, South, East

The Astrup Co.
2937 W. 25th St.
Cleveland, OH 44113
216-696-2820
Fax: 216-696-0977

Austram
1400 E. Geer St.
Durham, NC 27704
919-688-1288
1-800-966-1288

Fax: 919-688-0880

Avva Light Corp.
#5, 6025-12th St. S.E.
Calgary, AB T2H 2K1
Canada
403-252-6047
1-800-665-3749

Baja Products
4065 N. Romero Rd.
Tucson, AZ 85705
520-887-1154
1-800-845-2252
Fax: 520-888-5711

Baker Mfg. Corp.
4300-D LB McLeod Rd.
Orlando, FL 32811
407-649-3371
Fax: 407-246-0471

Balcon
P.O. Box 3388
2630 Conway Rd.
Crofton, MD 21114
301-721-1900
Fax: 301-793-0657

Bamboo & Rattan Works
470 Oberlin Ave. South
Lakewood, NJ 08701
732-370-0220
1-800-4-BAMBOO
Fax: 732-905-8386
E-mail:bambooman1@aol.com

Bark Plus
3 Old Mauldin Rd.
Greenville, SC 29607-4271
864-277-0717
Fax: 864-277-9029
Only in South

Barney's Ginseng Patch
433 Hwy. B
Montgomery City, MO 63361
573-564-2575

Barreto Manufacturing
66498 Highway 203
La Grande, OR 97850-5231
541-963-7348
1-800-525-7348
Fax: 541-963-6755
www.barretomfg.com

Barth Daylilies
71 Nelson Rd.
P.O. Box 54
Alna, ME 04535-0054

207-586-6455
www.tidewater.net/
~nsbarth

Basic Coatings
2124 Valley Dr.
Des Moines, IA 50321
515-288-0231
1-800-247-5471
Fax: 515-288-0615

BB&S Treated Lumber
Devil's Foot Rd.
P.O. Box 982
Davisville, RI 02854
401-884-0701
Fax: 401-295-9733

BC Greenhouse Builders
7425 Hedley Ave.
Burnaby, BC V5E 2R1
Canada
604-433-4220
Fax: 604-433-1285

Beacon Products
6503-E 19th St. E.
Sarasota, FL 34243
941-755-6694
Fax: 941-751-5535

Bear Cat/Crary Co.
P.O. Box 849
237 N.W. 12th St.
West Fargo, ND
58078-0849
701-282-5520
1-800-247-7335
Fax: 701-282-9522
www.crary.com

Bear Creek Nursery
P.O. Box 411
Northport, WA 99157
509-732-6219
Fax: 509-732-4417
www.bearcreeknursery.
com

Belden Brick Co.
700 Tuscarawas St. West
Canton, OH 44702-2024
330-456-0031
Fax: 330-456-2694
www.beldenbrick.com

Belson Outdoors
111 N. River Rd.
P.O. Box 207
North Aurora, IL 60542
630-897-8489
1-800-323-5664
Fax: 630-897-0573
www.belson.com

Bend Industries
11412 W. Brown Deer Rd.
Milwaukee, WI 53224
414-362-7000
Fax: 414-362-7009
Only in Midwest

Bend-A-Lite
6292 Windlass Cir.
Boynton Beach, FL 33437
407-738-5300
1-800-353-9636
Fax: 407-738-5055
www.bendalite.com

Benjamin Moore & Co.
51 Chestnut Ridge Rd.
Montvale, NJ 07645
201-573-9600
Fax: 201-573-6673
www.benjaminmoore.com

Benner's Gardens
P.O. Box 875
Bala Cynwyd, PA 19004
1-800-244-3337
Fax: 215-477-9429
www.bennersgardens.com

Berry Hill Limited
75 Burwell Rd.
St. Thomas, ON N5P 3R5
CANADA
519-631-0480
1-800-668-3072
Fax: 519-631-8935
www.berryhill.on.ca.

Bio-Gard Agronomics
P.O. Box 4477
Falls Church, VA 22044
703-356-1094
1-800-673-8502

BioLogic
Springtown Rd.
P.O. Box 177
Willow Hill, PA 17271
717-349-2789

BioTherm Hydronic, Inc.
P.O. Box 750967
Petaluma, CA 94975
707-794-9660
1-800-GETHEAT
Fax: 707-794-9663
E-mail:biotherm@getheat.
com

Bird Rock Tropicals
6523 El Camino Real
Carlsbad, CA 92009
760-438-9393
Fax: 760-438-1316
www.birdrocktropicals.
com

Bird-X
300 N. Elizabeth St.
Chicago, IL 60607
312-226-2473
Fax: 312-226-2480
E-mail:birdxinc@aol.com

BiWood Flooring
P.O. Box 17276
5744 Nanjack Cir.
Memphis, TN 38187-0276
901-795-3567
1-800-677-9663
Fax: 901-795-5348
E-mail:biwoodmphs@aol
.com

Bloomingfields Farm
Rt. 55
Gaylordsville, CT 06755
860-354-6951
www.
bloomingfieldsfarm.com

Bluebird International
1400 E. 66th Ave.
Denver, CO 80029
303-781-4458
1-800-808-BIRD
Fax: 303-781-1873
www.bluebirdintl.com

Bluestem Prairie Nursery
13197 E. 13th Rd.
Hillsboro, IL 62049
217-532-6344
E-mail:bluestem@cillnet.
com

Boiardi Products Corp.
453 Main St.
Little Falls, NJ 07424
973-256-1100
1-800-352-8668
Fax: 973-256-5744
Only in South, East

Bomanite Corp.
P.O. Box 599
Madera, CA 93639
209-673-2411
Fax: 209-673-8246
www.bomanite.com

Bon Tool Co.
4430 Gibsonia Rd.
Gibsonia, PA 15044
412-443-7080
1-800-444-7060
Fax: 412-443-7090

BonaKemi USA
14805 E. Moncrieff Pl.
Aurora, CO 80011-1207
303-371-1411
1-800-872-5515

Fax: 303-371-6958
www.bonakemi.com

Bondex Intl.
3616 Scarlet Oak Blvd.
St. Louis, MO 63122
314-225-5001
1-800-225-7522
Fax: 314-225-4159
www.bondex.com

Bonide Products
2 Wurz Ave.
Yorkville, NY 13495
315-736-8231
Fax: 315-762-5613
www.bonideproducts.com

Borbeleta Gardens
15980 Canby Ave.
Fairbault, MN 55021-7652
507-334-2807
Fax: 507-334-0365
E-mail:campbell@mears.
net

Bosmere
P.O. Box 363
Concord, NC 28026-0363
704-784-1608
Fax: 704-784-1611
www.easyweb.
easynet.co.uk/~bosmere

Boston Design Corp.
100 Magazine St.
Boston, MA 02119
617-442-6118
1-800-225-5584
Fax: 617-442-9633
www.members.aol.
.com/bdcorp/bdc.htm

Bountiful Gardens
18001 Shafer Ranch Rd.
Willits, CA 95490
707-459-6410
Fax: 707-459-6410
E-mail:bountiful@zapcom.
net

Bow House/Bowbends
P.O. Box 900
Bolton, MA 01740
978-779-6464
1-800-518-6471
Fax: 978-779-2272
www.bowbend.com

Brady Rooms
97 Webster St.
Worcester, MA 01603
508-755-9580
1-888-88-BRADY
Fax: 508-755-1284
www.bradyrooms.com

Brandon Industries
1601 W. Wilmeth Rd.
McKinney, TX 75069
972-542-3000
Fax: 972-542-1015
www.brandonmail.com

Brass Light Gallery
131 S. First St.
Milwaukee, WI 53204
1-800-243-9595
Fax: 414-271-7755

Brent and Becky's Bulbs
7463 Heath Trail
Gloucester, VA 23061
804-693-3966
Fax: 804-693-9436
E-mail:bbheath@aol.com

Brick Industry Assn.
11490 Commerce Park Dr.
Reston, VA 20191
703-620-0010
Fax: 703-620-3928
www.brickinfo.org

Brite Millwork
641 Hardwick Rd.
Bolton, ON L7E 5R2
Canada
905-857-6021
1-800-265-6021
Fax: 905-857-3211
Only in Midwest, South, East

Brochure Box Co.
1621 S.E. 28th Ter.
Cape Coral, FL 33904
941-945-7997
1-800-654-3753
Fax: 941-945-4621
www.brochurebox.com

Brock Deck Systems
Royal Crown Ltd.
P.O. Box 360
State Rd. 15 N.
Milford, IN 46542-0360
219-658-9442
1-800-365-3625
Fax: 219-658-3147
www.royalcrownltd.com

Brojack Lumber Co.
RD 1, Box 482
Olyphant, PA 18447
717-586-2281
Fax: 717-586-4627

Bronwood Worm Farms
P.O. Box 69
Bronwood, GA 31726
912-995-5994

Brooks Books

P.O. Box 91
Clayton, CA 94517-0091
925-672-4566
Fax: 925-672-3338
E-mail:brooksbk@netvista.net

Broyhill
P.O. Box 475
Dakota City, NE
68731-0475
402-987-3412
1-800-228-1003
Fax: 402-987-3601
www.broyhill.com

Bruce Hardwood Floors
(A Div. of Triangle Pacific Corp.)
16803 Dallas Pkwy.
Dallas, TX 75248-6196
214-887-2100
1-800-722-4647
Fax: 214-887-2234
www.brucehardwoodfloors.com

Bufftech
2525 Walden Ave.
Buffalo, NY 14225
716-685-1600
1-800-333-0569
Fax: 716-685-1172
www.bufftech.com

Builders Booksource
1817 Fourth St.
Berkeley, CA 94710
510-845-6874
1-800-843-2028
Fax: 510-845-7051
www.buildersbooksite.com

Builders Edge
P.O. Box 7739
Pittsburgh, PA 15215
412-782-4880
1-800-969-7245
Fax: 412-782-3314

The Bulb Crate
2560 Deerfield Rd.
Riverwoods, IL 60015
847-317-1414
Fax: 847-317-1417
E-mail:abulb@aol.com

Bulb Savers
P.O. Box 77216
West Trenton, NJ
08628-6216
609-883-6250
1-800-472-3284

Burlington Scientific Corp.
222 Sherwood Ave.
Farmingdale, NY 11735
516-694-9000
Fax: 516-694-9177
www.burlingtoncorp.com

Burnt Ridge Nursery
432 Burnt Ridge Rd.
Onalaska, WA 98570
360-985-2873
Fax: 360-985-0882
www.carow-ww.com/brnursery

The Burruss Co.
P.O. Box 6
103 Maddox St.
Brookneal, VA
24528-2907
804-376-2666
1-800-334-2495
Fax: 804-376-3698

Burt Associates Bamboo
P.O. Box 719
Westford, MA 01886
978-692-3240
Fax: 978-692-3222
www.tiac.net/users/bamboo

Burton Woodworks
(A Div. of MHJ Group)
4290 Alatex Rd.
Montgomery, AL 36108
334-281-0097
1-800-423-6589
Fax: 334-281-0336
www.mhjgroup.com

Busse Gardens
5873 Oliver Ave. S.W.
Cokato, MN 55321
320-286-2654
1-800-544-3192
Fax: 320-286-6601
E-mail:bussegardens@cmgate.com

Butler Box & Stake
3514 Westminster Ave.
Santa Ana, CA 92703
714-554-0600
1-800-666-0600
Fax: 714-554-0606

Butterbrooke Farm
78 Barry Rd.
Oxford, CT 06478-1529
203-888-2000

C & H Roofing
Country Cottage Roof
P.O. Box 2105
Lake City, FL 32056

904-755-1102
1-800-327-8115
Fax: 904-755-2353

Cabot
(Samuel Cabot Inc.)
100 Hale St.
Newburyport, MA 01950
978-465-1900
1-800-US-STAIN
Fax: 978-462-0511
www.cabotstain.com

Cactus by Dodie
934 Mettler Rd.
Lodi, CA 95242-9546
209-368-3692

Caladium World
P.O. Drawer 629
Sebring, FL 33871
941-385-7661
Fax: 941-385-5836

Caldera Spas & Baths
1080 W. Bradley Ave.
El Cajon, CA 92020
619-562-5120
1-800-669-1881
Fax: 619-562-7806

Calger Lighting
200 Lexington Ave.
Ste. 801
New York, NY 10016
212-689-9511
Fax: 212-779-0721

California Acrylic Industries/Cal Spas
1462 E. Ninth St.
Pomona, CA 91766
909-623-8781
1-800-CAL-SPAS
www.calspas.com

California Redwood Assn.
405 Enfrente Dr.
Suite 200
Novato, CA 94949
415-382-0662
1-888-CALREDWOOD
Fax: 415-382-8531
www.calredwood.org

Callahan Seeds
6045 Foley Ln.
Central Point, OR 97502
503-855-1164

Camellia Forest Nursery
125 Carolina Forest
Chapel Hill, NC 27516
919-968-0504
Fax: 919-967-5529
www.home.aol.com/camforest

Campberry Farms
RR 1
Niagara-on-the-Lake, ON
L0S 1J0 Canada
905-262-4927

Canadian Wildflower Society
P.O. Box 336, Station F
Toronto, ON M4Y 2L7
Canada
416-924-6807
www.acorn-online.com/
hedge/cws.html

Canaren (Palwa By Canaren)
255 Wildcat Rd.
North York, ON M3J 2S3
Canada
416-650-0309
1-800-361-3699
Fax: 416-650-0248

Cangelosi Marble and Granite
14021 W. Gessner
Missouri City, TX 77489
281-499-7521
Fax: 281-499-5315
www.cangelosi.com

Canital Granite
100 Hoka St.
Winnipeg, MB R2C 3N2
Canada
204-224-2286
1-800-665-0045
Fax: 204-222-8602

Cape Cod Worm Farm
30 Center Ave.
Buzzard's Bay, MA
02532-3145
508-759-5664
www.members.aol.
com/capeworms/
private/wormhome.htm

Cape Iris Gardens
822 Rodney Vista Blvd.
Cape Girardeau, MO
63701
573-334-3383

Carino Nurseries
P.O. Box 538, Dept. HP
Indiana, PA 15701
724-463-3350
1-800-223-7075
Fax: 724-463-3050
www.carinonurseries.com

Carlon Electrical Products
25701 Science Park Dr.
Cleveland, OH
44122-7313

216-831-4000
1-800-972-3462
Fax: 216-831-5579

Carlson's Garden's
Box 305
South Salem, NY 10590
914-763-5958
E-mail:bigazaleas@aol.com

Carmel Valley Seed Co.
P.O. Box 582
Carmel Valley, CA
93924-0582
Fax: 408-659-8028

Carolina Solar Structures
(A Div. of Bob Thompson Builders)
8 Loop Rd.
Arden, NC 28704
704-684-9900
1-800-241-9560
Fax: 704-684-9977
www.supplysite.com/
carolina-solar/

Cart Warehouse
P.O. Box 4
Point Arena, CA 95468
707-882-2001
1-888-882-2110
Fax: 707-882-2011
E-mail:peterr@mcn.org

Carts Vermont
1890 Airport Pkwy.
South Burlington, VT
05403-5875
802-862-6304
1-800-732-7417
Fax: 802-862-2304
www.together.net/~cartsvt

Cascade Forest Nursery
22033 Fillmore Rd.
Cascade, IA 52033
319-852-3042
Fax: 319-852-5004
www.cascadeforestry.com

Case Window & Door
301 Green St.
Schenectady, NY 12305
518-347-0614
1-800-227-3957
Fax: 518-347-0714

Cedarbrook Sauna
21326 Hwy. 9
Woodinville, WA 98072
509-782-2447
1-800-426-3929
Fax: 509-782-3680

Ceilings & Interior Systems Construction Assn.
1500 Lincoln Hwy.
Ste. 202
St. Charles, IL 60174
630-584-1919
1-800-524-7228
Fax: 630-584-2003
www.cisca.org

Centurion Products
1325 Sixth Ave. N.
Nashville, TN 37208-2603
615-256-6694
1-888-237-8762
Fax: 615-726-1795
www.centurionstone.com

Century Root Barriers
1401 N. Kraemer, Suite B
Anaheim, CA 92806
714-632-7083
1-800-480-8084
Fax: 714-632-5470

Cepco Tool
P.O. Box 153
Spencer, NY 14883
1-800-466-9626
Fax: 607-589-4313

CertainTeed Corp. Pipe & Plastics Group
Form-A-Drain
PO Box 860
750 E. Swedesford Rd.
Valley Forge, PA 19482
610-341-6950
Fax: 610-341-6837
www.certainteed.com

Chas. C. Hart Seed Co.
304 Main St.
P.O. Box 9169
Wethersfield, CT
06129-0169
860-529-2537
1-800-326-HART
Fax: 860-563-7221
www.hartseed.com

Chemque
22 Melanie Dr.
Brampton, ON L6T 4K9
Canada
416-679-5676
1-800-268-6111
Fax: 905-791-7525

Chimney King
P.O. Box 328
Gurnee, IL 60031
847-244-8860
Fax: 847-244-7970

Circle Redmont
2760 Business Center
Blvd.
Melbourne, FL 32940
407-259-7374
1-800-358-3888
Fax: 407-259-7237

Clargreen Gardens
814 Southdown Rd.
Mississauga, ON L5J 2Y4
Canada
905-822-0992
Fax: 905-822-7282

Classen Manufacturing
P.O. Box 172
Norfolk, NE 68702-0172
402-371-2294
1-888-252-7710
Fax: 402-371-3602

Classic Lamp Posts
3645 N.W. 67th St.
Miami, FL 33147
305-696-1901
1-800-654-5852
Fax: 305-836-1296
www.rotocast.com/classic

Classic Post & Beam
P.O. Box 546
York, ME 03909
1-800-872-2326
Fax: 207-363-2411
E-mail:classic14@aol.com

Classy Glass Structures
344 McDonnell
Lewisville, TX 75057
972-221-0445
Fax: 972-219-0348

Cleform Tool Co.- Owens Pro Line
4343 Easton Rd.
St. Joseph, MO 64503
816-233-4840
1-800-253-3676
Fax: 816-233-4624
www.ccp.com/~cleform

Clinton Street Greenhouse
5175 Clinton Street Rd.
Batavia, NY 14020-1132
716-345-9319
E-mail:flowerguy007@
webtv.net

Cloud Forest Orchids
P.O. Box 370
Honokaa, HI 96727
808-987-4492

Coastal Lumber Co./
(Treated Products Div.)
P.O. Drawer 1207
Uniontown, PA 15401
724-438-3527
Fax: 724-438-4202
www.coastallumber.com
Only in Midwest, South, East

Cold Stream Farm
2030 Free Soil Rd.
Free Soil, MI 49411
616-464-5809

Colorblends by Schipper & Co.
Box 7584
Greenwich, CT 06836
1-888-TIP-TOES
Fax: 203-862-8909
www.colorblends.com

Columbia Mfg. Co.
3845 William St.
Burnaby, BC V5C 3J1
Canada
604-294-5231
Fax: 604-294-5120

Colvos Creek Nursery
P.O. Box 1512
Vashon Island, WA 98070
206-749-9508
Fax: 206-463-3917
E-mail:colvoscreek@juno.com

Comanche Acres Iris Gardens
12421 S.E. St. Rt. 116
Gower, MO 64454
816-424-6436
1-800-382-4747
Fax: 816-424-3836
E-mail:comancheacres@juno.com

Combustion Service
P.O. Box 40
140 W. Myers Blvd.
Mascotte, FL 34753-0040
352-429-4740
1-800-503-3310
Fax: 352-429-4977
www.agricarts.com

Commonwealth Solar Rooms
P.O. Box 15035
3401 Industrial Dr.
Durham, NC 27704
919-620-6830
1-800-870-6830
Fax: 919-620-8665
Only in Midwest, South, East

Companion Plants
7247 N. Coolville Ridge Rd.
Athens, OH 45701
740-592-4643
Fax: 740-593-3092
www.frognet.net/companion_plants/

Comstock Seed
8520 W. 4th St.
Reno, NV 89523
702-746-3681
Fax: 702-746-1701

Concrete Designs
3650 S. Broadmont Dr.
Tucson, AZ 85713
520-624-6653
1-800-279-2278
Fax: 520-624-3420

The Conservancy
51563 Range Rd. 212A
Sherwood Park, AB
T8G 1B1
Fax: 780-434-7401
www.icangarden.com

Consolidated Coatings Corp.
2614 Pearl Rd., PO Box 10
Brunswick, OH 44212
330-220-6754
1-800-321-7886
Fax: 330-220-6761

Contemporary Structures
1102 Center St.
Ludlow, MA 01056
413-589-0147
Fax: 413-589-1572

Continental Industries
100 Summerlea Rd.
Brampton, ON L6T 4X3
Canada
905-792-9330
Fax: 905-792-8996

Cooley's Strawberry Nursery
P.O. Box 472
Augusta, AR 72006
870-347-2026
Zip: 44273-9413
www.cropking.com

Cotter's Tree Service
10662 Court Ave.
Stanton, CA 90680-2459
714-527-3600
1-800-416-9438
Fax: 714-821-5241
www.texomaonline.com/ces

Country Casual
9085 Comprint Ct.
Gaithersburg, MD 20877
1-800-284-8325
Fax: 301-926-9198
www.countrycasual.com

Country Home Products
25 Meigs Rd.
Vergennes, VT 05491
1-800-446-8746

Craft-Bilt Mfg. Co.
53 Souderton-Hatfield Pike
Souderton, PA 18964
215-721-7700
1-800-422-8577
Fax: 215-721-9338
www.craftbilt.com

Crane Plastics Co.
PO Box 1047
Columbus, OH 43216
614-443-4891
1-800-307-7780
Fax: 614-443-1436
www.timbertech.com

Creative Building Products
(A Div. of Spirit of America Corp.)
4307 Arden Dr.
Fort Wayne, IN 46804-4400
219-459-0456
1-800-860-2855
Fax: 219-459-0929

Creative Structures
281 N. West End Blvd.
Quakertown, PA 18951-2046
215-538-2426
1-800-873-3966
Fax: 215-538-7308

Crop King
5050 Greenwich Rd.
Seville, OH 44273-9413
330-769-2002
1-800-321-5656
Fax: 330-769-2616
www.cropking.com

Crosman Seed Corp.
P.O. Box 110
East Rochester, NY 14445
716-586-1928
1-800-446-SEED
1-716-586-6093

Cross Vinylattice
3174 Marjan Dr.
Atlanta, GA 30340
770-451-4531
1-800-521-9878

Fax: 770-457-5125

Cultured Stone Corp.
P.O. Box 270
Napa, CA 94559
707-255-1727
1-800-255-1727
Fax: 707-255-5572
www.culturedstone.com

Cumberland Woodcraft
P.O. Drawer 609
10 Stover Dr.
Carlisle, PA 17013
717-243-0063
1-800-367-1884
Fax: 717-243-6502
www.pa.net/cwc

Cummins Garden
22 Robertsville Rd.
Marlboro, NJ 07746
732-536-2591

Cuprinol
101 Prospect Ave.
Cleveland, OH 44115
216-566-3131
Fax: 216-566-1655
www.cuprinol.com

Curt Bean Lumber Co.
P.O. Box 200
Glenwood, AR 71943
870-356-4165
1-800-232-2326
Fax: 870-356-4100

CYRO
6285 Northam Dr.
Ste. 100
Mississauga, ON L4V 1X5
Canada
1-800-461-7398
Fax: 905-677-7805
www.cyro.com

The Daffodil Mart
30 Irene St.
Torrington, CT 06790
06790-6668
1-800-255-2852
Fax: 800-420-2852

Dakota Granite
P.O. Box 1351
Milbank, SD 57252
605-432-5580
1-800-843-3333
Fax: 800-338-5346
Fax: 605-432-6155

Dalen Products
11110 Gilbert Dr.
Knoxville, TN 37932-3099
423-966-3256
1-800-747-3256
Fax: 423-966-6404

Dalton Pavillions
20 Commerce Dr.
Telford, PA 18969
215-721-1492

Daly's Wood Finishing Products
3525 Stone Way Ave. N.
Seattle, WA 98103
206-633-4200
1-800-735-7019
Fax: 206-632-2565

Dampney Co.
85 Paris St.
Everett, MA 02149-4421
617-389-2805
1-800-537-7023
Fax: 617-380-0484

DAP
855 N. Third St.
P.O. Box 277
Dayton, OH 45401-0277
513-667-4461
1-800-543-3840
Fax: 513-667-3331

David Bacon Fine Handcrafted Furniture
16698 Fritillary Way
Grass Valley, CA 95945
530-273-8889
Fax: 530-273-7928

Davidson Wilson Greenhouses
RR 2, Box 168, Dept. 11
Crawfordsville, IN 47933
765-364-0556
Fax: 765-364-0563
www.davidson-wilson.com

Dawes Engine Generator
224 Boston St.
Topsfield, MA 01983-2220
978-887-5045
1-800-649-5045
Fax: 978-887-3094

Day-Dex Co.
4725 N.W. 36th Ave.
Miami, FL 33142
305-635-5241

Daylily Discounters
One Daylily Plaza
Alachua, FL 32615
904-462-1539
Fax: 904-462-5111
www.daylilydiscounters.com

De Witt Co.
RR 3 Box 31
85 De Witt Dr.

Sikeston, MO 63801-9302
573-472-0048
1-800-888-9669
Fax: 573-471-6715
www.dewittco.com

Dean & Barry
970 Woodland Ave.
Columbus, OH 43219
614-258-3131
1-800-325-2829
Fax: 614-258-3530
E-mail:mdshapiro@bigfoot.com

DEC-K-ING
1160 Yew Ave, Suite 84
Blaine, WA 98231
1-800-804-6288
Fax: 604-530-4466
www.dec-k-ing.com

Decor Grates
114 Bows Rd., Unit No. 1
Concorde, ON L4K 1J8
Canada
905-669-1218
1-800-903-9036
Fax: 800-362-0923
www.decorgrate.com

DecTec
4500 8A St. N.E.
Calgary, AB T2E 4J7
Canada
403-277-0700
1-800-268-1078
Fax: 403-277-4373
E-mail:skygroup@telusplanet.net

Dee Sign Co.
6163 Allen Rd.
Cincinnati, OH 45069
513-779-3333
1-800-DEE-SIGN
Fax: 513-779-3344

Deep Root
345 Lorton Ave.
Suite 103
Burlingame, CA 94010
650-344-1464
1-800-458-7668
Fax: 650-344-9380
www.deeproot.com

DeGiorgi Seed Co.
6011 'N' St.
Omaha, NE 68117
402-731-3901
1-800-858-2580
Fax: 402-731-8475

Delmarva Lawn & Power Equipment
36295 Old Ocean City Rd.
Willards, MD 21874-1120
410-835-2727

Dependable Chemical Co.
P.O. Box 16334
Rocky River, OH
44116-0334
440-333-1123
1-800-227-3434
Fax: 440-333-0070
www.floorprep.com

Desertland Nursery
11306 Gateway East
El Paso, TX 79927-7701
915-858-1130
Fax: 915-858-1560

Diedrich Technologies
7373 S. Sixth St.
Oak Creek, WI 53154
414-764-0058
1-800-323-3565
Fax: 414-764-6993

Digger's Product Development Co.
P.O. Box 1551
Soquel, CA 95073
831-462-6095
Fax: 831-464-1825
E-mail:digger@pacbell.net

Direct Edge
1480 Arrow Hwy.
La Verne, CA 91750-5219
909-392-4646

Dixon Industries
P.O. Box 1569
Coffeyville, KS
67337-0945
316-251-2000
Fax: 316-251-4117
www.dixon-ztr.com

DM Industries/Vita Intl.
2320 N.W. 147th St.
Miami, FL 33054
305-688-5739
1-800-BUY VITA
Fax: 305-688-9415

Donovan's Roses
P.O. Box 37800
Shreveport, LA 71133
318-865-3273

Dorothy Biddle Service
348 Greeley Lake Rd.
Greeley, PA 18425
717-226-3239
Fax: 717-226-0349
www.dorothybiddle.com

Dramm Corporation
P.O. Box 1960
Manitowoc, WI

54221-1960
920-684-0227
1-800-258-0848
Fax: 920-684-4499

Dreamscape Lighting Mfg.
10610 Culver Blvd.
Culver City, CA 90232
310-838-7043
Fax: 310-202-8536
E-mail:dreamscape@globalpac.com

DripWorks
231 East San Francisco St.
Willits, CA 95490
707-459-6323
1-800-616-8321
Fax: 707-459-9645
www.dripworksusa.com

Duckback Products
Superdeck Brand Products
P.O. Box 980
644 Hegan Ln.
Chico, CA 95928
530-343-3261
1-800-825-5382
Fax: 530-343-3283
www.superdeck.com

Duo-Gard Industries
40442 Koppernick Rd.
Canton, MI 48187
313-207-9700
1-800-872-4404
Fax: 313-207-7995
www.duo-gard.com

Dura Seal
(Div. of Minwax Co.)
P.O. Box 783
Upper Saddle River, NJ
07458-0783
201-391-0253
1-800-526-0495

Dura-Bilt Products
P.O. Box 188
Wellsburg, NY 14894
717-596-2000
1-800-233-4251
Fax: 717-596-3296
Only in Midwest, South, East

Dur-A-Flex
P.O. Box 280166
East Hartford, CT
06128-0166
860-528-9838
1-800-253-3539
Fax: 860-528-2802

DuraVinyl
1576 Magnolia Dr.
Macon, MS 39341
1-888-283-4893

Fax: 601-726-9856
E-mail:odtech@ebicom.net

**Dutch Boy
Professional Paints**
101 Prospect Ave.
Cleveland, OH 44115
216-566-2929
1-800-828-5669
Fax: 216-566-2771

Dutch Gardens
P.O. Box 200
Adelphia, NJ 07710
1-800-818-3861
Fax: 732-780-7720
www.dutchgardens.nl

**D.V. Burrell Seed
Growers Co.**
P.O. Box 150-LGG
Rocky Ford, CO 81067
719-254-3318
Fax: 719-254-3319

Dyco Paints
5850 Ulmerton Rd.
Clearwater, FL 33760
813-536-6560
1-800-237-8232
Fax: 813-536-0561
Only in South

**Dyna-Gro Nutrition
Solutions**
1065 Broadway
San Pablo, CA 94806
510-233-0254
1-800-DYNA-GRO
Fax: 510-233-0198
www.dynagro.com

Eagle Electric Mfg. Co.
45-31 Court Sq.
Long Island City, NY
  11101
718-937-8000
1-800-441-3177
Fax: 718-482-0160
Fax: 800-329-3055
www.eagle-electric.com

**Earl May Seed &
Nursery**
208 Elm St.
Shenandoah, IA 51603
712-246-1020
Fax: 712-246-2210
www.earlmay.com

Earthly Goods
P.O. Box 614
New Albany, IN 47150
812-944-2903
Fax: 812-944-2903
www.earthlygoods.com

**Earthstone Retaining
Wall Systems**
784 Butterfield Ln.
San Marcos, CA 92069
619-740-9370
Fax: 619-740-9399

Easy Gardener
P.O. Box 21025
Waco, TX 76702-1025
254-753-5353
1-800-327-9462
Fax: 254-753-5372
www.easygardener.com

Eclipse Lighting
3123 N. Pulaski Rd.
Chicago, IL 60641
773-481-9161
Fax: 773-481-0729
E-mail:cigcom.net

Edible Landscaping
P.O. Box 77
Afton, VA 22920
804-361-9134
1-800-524-4156
Fax: 804-361-1916
www.eat-it.com

Eldorado Stone Corp.
P.O. Box 489
Carnation, WA 98014
425-333-6722
1-800-925-1491
Fax: 425-333-4755
www.eldoradostone.com

Elements
4920 Otter Lake Rd.
White Bear Lake, MN
  55110
612-653-7745
1-800-223-2788
Fax: 612-653-3575

**Elisabeth Woodburn,
Books, ABAA**
P.O. Box 398
Hopewell, NJ 08525
609-466-0522
E-mail:qege21a@prodigy.
com

Elixir Farm Botanicals
General Delivery
Brixey, MO 65618
417-261-2393
1-877-315-SEED
Fax: 417-261-2355
www.elixirfarm.com

Emi Meade, Importer
16000 Fern Way
Guerneville, CA
95446-9322
707-869-3218
Fax: 707-869-3218
www.gardenclogs.com

**Ensurco Duradek
(U.S.)**
404 E. 13th Ave.
N. Kansas City, MO
64116-4035
816-421-5830
1-800-338-3568
Fax: 816-421-2924
www.duradek.com

**Evergreen Systems
Sunrooms**
P.O. Box 293
Beaver Dam, WI 53916
414-485-4848
1-800-775-1237
Fax: 414-485-4949

Excel Industries
P.O. Box 7000
Hesston, KS 67062-2097
316-327-4911
1-800-395-4757
Fax: 316-327-3123
www.excelhustler.com

**E-Z Deck—
Pultronex Corp.**
2305 Eighth St.
Nisku, AB T9E 7Z3
Canada
403-955-7374
1-800-990-3099
Fax: 403-955-7170
www.ezdeck.com

Fancy Fronds
P.O. Box 1090
Gold Bar, WA 98251
360-793-1472

**Farm Wholesale
Greenhouses**
3740 Brooklake Rd. N.E.
Salem, OR 97303
503-393-3973
1-800-825-1925
Fax: 503-393-3119
www.farmwholesale.com

FC Lighting
1113 N. Main St.
Lombard, IL 60148
708-889-8100
1-800-900-1730
Fax: 708-889-8106

**Federal Wood
Products**
409 Highland Ave.
Middletown, NY 10940
914-342-1511
1-800-342-1514

**Feder's Prairie
Seed Co.**
12871 380th Ave.
Blue Earth, MN 56013

507-526-3049
Fax: 507-526-3509
E-mail:feder@bevcomm.
net
Only in Midwest

**Feeney Wire Rope &
Rigging**
P.O. Box 23805
Oakland, CA 94623-0805
510-839-7343
1-800-888-2418
Fax: 510-893-9484
www.feeneywire.com

Fehrman Industries
14955 Grover St.
Omaha, NE 68144-3237
402-334-3434
1-800-204-3535
Fax: 402-334-3407

Fero Corp.
15305-117 Ave.
Edmonton, AB T5M 3X4
Canada
403-455-5098
Fax: 403-452-5969

Fiberglass Access
841 Helm Ave., N.W.
Palm Bay, FL 32907-7798
407-729-1426
Fax: 407-729-1426

Fiberstars
2883 Bayview Dr.
Fremont, CA 94538
1-800-327-7877
Fax: 510-490-3247
www.fiberstars.com

**Field and Forest
Products**
N3296 Kozuzek Rd.
Peshtigo, WI 54157-9610
715-582-4997
1-800-792-6220
Fax: 715-582-0181
E-mail:ffp@mari.net

Fieldstone Gardens
620 Quaker Ln.
Vassalboro, ME
04989-9713
207-923-3836
Fax: 207-923-3836
www.
fieldstonegardens.com

Fine Paints of Europe
P.O. Box 419, Rt. 4 W.
Woodstock, VT
05091-0419
802-457-2468
1-800-332-1556
Fax: 802-457-3984
www.fine-paints.com

Firestone Building Prod. Co.
PondGard Rubber Liners
525 Congressional Blvd.
Carmel, IN 46032
317-575-7095
1-800-428-4442 ext. 7095
Fax: 317-575-7002
www.firestonebpco.com

Fiskars Lawn & Garden Div
780 Carolina St.
Sauk City, WI 53583-1369
608-643-4389

The Flecto Co.
1000 45th St.
Oakland, CA 94608-3398
510-655-2470
1-800-635-3286
Fax: 510-652-7135

Flexi-Wall Systems
(A Div. of Wall & Floor Treatments)
P.O. Box 89
Liberty, SC 29657
864-843-3104
1-800-843-5394
Fax: 864-843-9318

Flickinger's Nursery
P.O. Box 245
Sagamore, PA 16250
1-800-368-7381

The Flood Co.
P.O. Box 2535
1212 Barlow Rd.
Hudson, OH 44236-0035
330-656-3033
1-800-321-3444
Fax: 330-650-1453
www.floodco.com

Florian Greenhouse
64 Airport Rd.
West Milford, NJ 07480
201-728-7800
1-800-FLORIAN
Fax: 201-728-3206

Florian Ratchet-Cut Pruning Tools
P.O. Box 325
Plantsville, CT 06479
860-628-9643
1-800-275-3618
Fax: 860-628-6036

Florida Colors Nursery
23740 S.W. 147th Ave.
Homestead, FL 33032-2112
305-258-1086
Fax: 305-258-6317
E-mail:luc.vannoorbeeck2@

gte.com
Only in South

Florida Mycology Research Center
P.O. Box 8104
Pensacola, FL 32505
850-327-4378
E-mail:72253,1553@
compuserve.com

Florikan Southeast
P.O. Box 2115
Semmes, AL 36575-2115
334-645-9847
1-800-552-8666
Fax: 334-645-9851
Only in South

Flos USA
200 McKay Rd.
Huntington Station, NY 11746
516-549-2745
Fax: 516-549-4220

Flo-Well Water Management
1600 Falmouth Rd.
Suite 1
Centerville, MA 02632-2939
508-790-3266
1-800-356-9935
Fax: 508-790-0083
www.flowell.com

Forestfarm
990 Tetherow Rd.
Williams, OR 97544
541-846-6963
Fax: 541-846-6963
www.forestfarm.com

ForestLake Gardens
Box 535, HC 72, Low
Locust Grove, VA 22508-9550
540-972-2890
E-mail:tamarac@erols.com

Formglas
20 Toro Rd.
North York, ON M3J 2A7
Canada
416-635-8030
Fax: 416-635-6588
www.formglas.com

Forms + Surfaces
6395 Cindy Ln.
Carpinteria, CA 93013
805-684-8626
1-800-451-0410
Fax: 805-684-8620
www.forms-surfaces.com

Four Seasons Solar Products
5005 Veterans Memorial Hwy.
Holbrook, NY 11741
516-563-4000
1-800-FOUR-SEASONS
Fax: 516-563-4010
www.four-seasons-sunrooms.com

Fox Hill Nursery
347 Lunt Rd.
Freeport, ME 04032
207-729-1511
Fax: 207-729-6108
www.lilacs.com

Fred's Plant Farm
4589 Ralston Rd.
Martin, TN 38237
1-800-550-2575

Freshops
36180 Kings Valley Hwy.
Philomath, OR 97370
541-929-2736
Fax: 541-929-2702
www.freshops.com

Frey's Dahlias
12054 Brick Rd.
Turner, OR 97392
E-mail:freydahlia@juno.com

Friendship Gardens
341 Schwartz Rd.
Gettysburg, PA 17325-8622
717-338-1657
Fax: 717-338-0247
E-mail:joan@cvn.net

Frosty Holly Ecological Restoration
Box 53
Langley, WA 98260
360-579-2332
Fax: 360-579-2332
E-mail:wean@whidbey.net

FSI Home Products Div.
Flotation Systems
2700 Alabama Hwy. 69 S.
Cullman, AL 35057
205-287-0417
1-800-711-1785
Fax: 205-287-0417

Fypon
22 W. Pennsylvania Ave.
P.O. Box 365
Stewartstown, PA 17363
717-993-2593
1-800-537-5349
Fax: 717-993-3782
www.fypon.com

G & R Trellis & Supply Co.
6250 W. Atlantic Ave.
Delray Beach, FL 33484-3551
561-499-2655 ext. 111
Fax: 561-496-0952
E-mail:prosacker@aol.com

Garden Essence
1576 Magnolia Dr.
Macon, MS 39341

Garden of Delights
14560 S.W. 14th St.
Davie, FL 33325
954-370-9004
1-800-741-3103
Fax: 954-236-4588
www.gardenofdelights.com

Garden Perennials
Rt. 1, Box 164
Wayne, NE 68787
402-375-3615
E-mail:gkorn@bloomnet.com

Garden Place
P.O. Box 388
Mentor, OH 44061
440-255-3705
Fax: 440-255-9535

Gardens of the Blue Ridge
P.O. Box 10
Pineola, NC 28662
828-733-2417
Fax: 828-733-8894

Garland Commercial Industries
185 E. South St.
Freeland, PA 18224
717-636-1000
1-800-25-RANGE
Fax: 717-636-2713

GE Lighting
Nela Park
Cleveland, OH 44112
216-266-2121
1-800-GE-LAMPS
www.ge.com

GE Lighting Systems
3010 Spartanburg Hwy.
Hendersonville, NC 28739
704-693-2000
1-800-626-2004
Fax: 518-869-2828
www.ge.com

General Shale Brick
P.O. Box 3547
Johnson City, TN 37602

423-282-4661
1-800-414-4661
Fax: 423-952-4104
www.generalshale.com

Genie House
P.O. Box 2478
Vincentown, NJ 08088
609-859-0600
1-800-634-3643
Fax: 609-859-0565

Genova Products
P.O. Box 309
7034 E. Court St.
Davison, MI 48423-0309
810-744-4500
1-800-521-7488
Fax: 810-658-1815
www.genovaproducts.com

Geocel Corp.
53280 Marina Dr.
Elkhart, IN 46514
219-264-0645
1-800-348-7615
Fax: 219-264-3698
E-mail:geocel@aol.com

Gerber Industries
1 Gerber Industrial Dr.
P.O. Box 610
St. Peters, MO
63376-0610
314-278-5710
1-800-844-1401
Fax: 314-278-4727

Gibco Services
725 S. Adams Rd.
Ste. L-59
Birmingham, MI 48009
248-647-3322
Fax: 248-647-8720

Gibson-Homans Co.
1755 Enterprise Pkwy.
Twinsburg, OH 44087
216-425-3255
1-800-433-7293
Fax: 216-425-2546

**Gilbert H. Wild
and Son**
3044 State Hwy. 37
P.O. Box 338
Sarcoxie, MO 64862
417-548-3514
1-888-GHWILDS
Fax: 888-548-6831
E-mail:wilds@socket.com

Glen-Gery Corp.
1166 Spring St.
P.O. Box 7001
Wyomissing, PA 19610
610-374-4011
Fax: 610-374-1622
www.glengerybrick.com

**Golden Lake
Greenhouses**
10782 Citrus Dr.
Moorpark, CA 93021
E-mail:goldenlake1@juno.
com

Good Seed Co.
P.O. Box 1485
Tonasket, WA 98855
509-486-1047
www.planettonasket.com/
goodseed

**Goodwin Creek
Gardens**
P.O. Box 83
Williams, OR 97544
541-846-7357

The Gordon Corp.
170 Spring St.
Southington, CT 06489
860-628-0000
1-800-333-4564
Fax: 860-621-1251
www.gordoncelladoor.com

Gossler Farms Nursery
1200 Weaver Rd.
Springfield, OR 97478
541-746-3922
Fax: 541-744-7924

**Gothic Arch
Greenhouses**
(A Div. of Trans-Sphere
Trading Corp.)
PO Box 1564
Mobile, AL 36633
334-432-7529
1-800-628-4974

**The Gourmet
Gardener**
8650 College Blvd.
Dept. 205-SK
Overland Park, KS 66210
913-345-0490
Fax: 913-451-2443
www.
gourmetgardener.com

**Gourmet Mushroom
Products**
P.O. Box 515
Graton, CA 95444
707-829-7301
1-800-789-9121
Fax: 707-823-9091
www.gmushrooms.com

**Grabber Construction
Products**
205 Mason Cir.
Concord, CA 94520
510-680-0777
1-800-477-TURN
Fax: 510-687-6261

Grani-Decor Tiles
1040 Rue Bussiere
St. Sebastien, PQ
G0Y 1M0 Canada
819-652-2361
Fax: 819-652-2360
www.grani-decor.com

Grasshopper Co.
105 Old 81 Hwy.
Moundridge, KS
67107-7110
316-345-8621
Fax: 316-345-2301
www.
grasshoppermower.com

**Great Southern Wood
Preserving**
P.O. Box 610, Hwy. 431 N.
Abbeville, AL 36310
334-585-2291
Fax: 334-585-3683
Internet: http://www.
greatsouthernwood.com

**Greenheart-
Durawoods**
P.O. Box 279
Bayville, NJ 08721
908-269-6400
1-800-783-7220
Fax: 908-269-9797
E-mail:paulope@aol.com

**Greenthumb Daylily
Gardens**
1315 E. Rollingwood Cir.
Winston-Salem, NC 27105
336-377-2975

Grimo Nut Nursery
979 Lakeshore Rd., RR 3
Niagara-on-the-Lake, ON
L0S 1J0 Canada
905-934-6887 (YEH-
NUTS)

Growers Supply
P.O. Box 219
Dexter, MI 48130
734-426-5852
1-800-426-3885
E-mail:growers@aol.com

The Guano Co. Intl.
3562 E. 80th St.
Cleveland, OH
44105-1522
216-641-1200
1-800-4-B-GUANO
Fax: 216-641-1310

Guth Lighting
2615 Washington St.
P.O. Box 7079
St. Louis, MO 63177
314-533-3200
Fax: 314-533-9127

H & C Concrete Stain
101 Prospect Ave., N.W.
Cleveland, OH 44115
216-566-2000
1-800-TO-STAIN
Fax: 216-566-1832

Haddonstone (USA)
201 Heller Pl.
Interstate Business Park
Bellmawr, NJ 08031
609-931-7011
Fax: 609-931-0040

Halo Lighting
(A Brand of Cooper
Lighting)
400 Busse Rd.
Elk Grove Village, IL
60007
708-956-8400
Fax: 708-956-1537

Hamlet & Garneau
933 Michelin
Laval, PQ H7L 5B6
Canada
514-629-1776
Fax: 514-629-1197

Handy Home Products
6400 E. 11 Mile Rd.
Warren, MI 48901
810-757-2828
1-800-221-1849
Fax: 810-757-6066

Hanover Lantern
470 High St.
Hanover, PA 17331
717-632-6464
Fax: 717-632-5039
E-mail:hanoverlantern@
sun-link.com

**Hardscrabble
Enterprises**
P.O. Box 1124
Franklin, WV 26807-1124
304-358-2921
Fax: 304-358-2921

**Harris Specialty
Chemicals**
(Formerly Hydrozo,
Thoro, Watson Bowman
Acme, Selby)
10245 Centurion Pkwy. N.
Jacksonville, FL
32256-0564
904-996-6000
Fax: 904-996-6300

**Hartford
Conservatories**
96A Commerce Way
Woburn, MA 01801
617-937-9050

1-800-963-8700
Fax: 617-937-9025
www.hartford~con.com

**Hauser's Superior
View Farm**
Rt. 1, Box 199
Bayfield, WI 54814
715-779-5404
Fax: 715-779-5424

Heaths and Heathers
502 E. Haskell Hill Rd.
Shelton, WA 98584-8429
360-427-5318
Fax: 360-427-5318
www.
heathsandheathers.com

**Heckendorn
Equipment**
P.O. Box 134
Peabody, KS 66866-0134
316-983-2186
1-800-835-7805
Fax: 316-983-2880

Heinze Plant Labels
1840 17th Ave.
Santa Cruz, CA
95062-1862
831-475-0429
Fax: 831-475-1528

Heirloom Seeds
P.O. Box 245
West Elizabeth, PA 15088
412-384-0852
Fax: 412-384-0852
www.heirloomseeds.com

Heritage Finishes
1635 Sismet Rd., Unit 26
Mississauga, ON
L4W 1W5 Canada
905-271-9176
Fax: 905-271-4263

**Heritage Vinyl
Products**
1576 Magnolia Dr.
Macon, MS 39341
1-800-473-3623
Fax: 800-335-3991
www.heritagevinyl.com

Herwig Lighting
P.O. Box 768
Russellville, AR 72801
501-968-2621
1-800-643-9523
Fax: 501-968-6762
www.herwig.com

The Hess Mfg. Co.
P.O. Box 127
Quincy, PA 17247-0127
717-749-3141

1-800-541-6666
1-800-321-4377
Fax: 717-749-3712
Only in Midwest, South, East

.hessamerica
P.O. Box 430
Shelby, NC 28151
704-471-2211
Fax: 704-471-2255
www.hessamerica.com

Hickock Pruning Tools
200 S. Columbia St.
Wenatchee, WA
98801-3029
509-662-6065

**Hidden Springs
Nursery**
170 Hidden Springs Ln.
Cookeville, TN 38501

High-Lites
2142 Thomaston Ave.
Waterbury, CT 06704
203-575-2044
Fax: 203-574-3289

Hillary's Garden
29 Foley Rd.
Warwick, NY 10990-2823
914-987-1175
E-mail: hillarys@
warwick.net
Only in Midwest, South, East

Hildebrandt's Gardens
1710 Cleveland St.
Lexington, NE
68850-2721

Hinkley Lighting
12600 Berea Rd.
Cleveland, OH 44111
216-671-3300
1-800-446-5539
Fax: 216-671-4537

Historical Roses
1657 W. Jackson St.
Painesville, OH 44077
440-357-7270

Hoffco
358 N.W. F St.
Richmond, IN 47374
765-966-8161
1-800-999-8161
Fax: 765-935-2346
www.hoffcocomet.com

**Hoglund Landscape
Construction**
503 1/2 7th St. N.
Fargo, ND 58102
701-280-3149
1-800-882-8112

Holland Bulb Farms
P.O. Box 220
Tatamy, PA 18085
1-800-283-5082
Fax: 888-508-3762

Holland Gardens
29106 Meridian East
Graham, WA 98338
253-847-5425

**Holland Log Homes
Mfg. Co.**
13352 Van Buren St.
Holland, MI 49424
616-399-9627
Fax: 616-399-8530

**Holland Wildflower
Farm**
290 O'Neal Ln.
Elkins, AR 72727
501-643-2622
1-800-684-3734
Fax: 501-643-2249
Internet: http://www.
hwildflower.com

Holophane Corp.
250 E. Broad St.
Ste. 1400
Columbus, OH 43215
614-345-9631
Fax: 614-349-4426

Home Planners
3275 W. Ina Rd.
Suite 110
Tucson, AZ 85741
520-297-8200
Fax: 520-297-6219
www.homeplanners.com

Homestead Farms
3701 Highway EE
Owensville, MO 65066
573-437-4277
Fax: 573-437-4277

**Houses & Barns by
John Libby**
Barn Masters
P.O. Box 258H
Freeport, ME 04032
207-865-4169
1-800-869-4169
Fax: 207-865-6169
E-mail:johnlibby@aol.com

Hubbell Lighting
2000 Electric Way
Christiansburg, VA
24073-2500
540-382-6111
Fax: 540-382-1526

Hughes Nursery
1305 Wynooche West
Montesano, WA 98563
360-249-3702
Fax: 360-249-5580
E-mail:grhoward@
techline.com

Hunter Fan Co.
2500 Frisco Ave.
Memphis, TN 38114
901-743-1360
Fax: 901-745-9385
www.hunterfan.com

**Hy Grade Planting
Mix**
25200 Vermont Ave.
Harbor City, CA
90710-3120
310-326-6996

Hydro Turf
1340 Sibley Memorial
  Hwy.
Mendota, MN 55150-1414
612-452-9230
Fax: 612-452-6749

ICI Paint Stores
925 Euclid Ave.
Cleveland, OH 44115
216-344-8636
1-800-984-5444
Fax: 216-344-8883

Idaho Wood
P.O. Box 488
Sandpoint, ID 83864
208-263-9521
1-800-635-1100
Fax: 208-263-3102
www.idahowood.com

Increte Systems
8509 Sunstate St.
Tampa, FL 33634
813-886-8811
1-800-752-4626
Fax: 813-886-0188
www.increte.com

**Ingersoll Equipment
Co.**
200 Ingersoll Rd.
P.O. Box 5001
Winneconne, WI 54986
920-582-5000
1-800-880-6421

**Insulated Building
Systems**
22377 Cedar Green Rd.
Ste. 2B
Dulles, VA 20166
703-450-4886
Fax: 703-450-6642
Only in South, East

IntAgra Deer-away
8500 Pillsbury Ave. S.
Minneapolis, MN 55420
612-881-5535
1-800-468-2472
Fax: 612-881-7002

Integrated Fertiltiy Management
33 Ohme Gardens Rd.
Wenatchee, WA 98801
509-662-3179
1-800-332-3179
Fax: 509-662-6594

Intelectron
21021 Corsair Blvd.
Hayward, CA 94545-1301
510-732-6790
Fax: 510-732-6910

International Cast Polymer Assn.
8201 Greensboro Dr.
Ste. 300
McLean, VA 22102
703-610-9034
1-800-414-4272
Fax: 703-610-9005
www.icpa-hq.com

International Energy Systems
P.O. Box 588
Barrington, IL 60011
708-381-0203
1-800-927-0419
Fax: 708-381-3997

International Irrigation Systems
P.O. Box 360
Niagara Falls, NY 14304
905-688-4090
Fax: 905-688-4093
www.irrigro.com

International Oleander Society
P.O. Box 3431
Galveston, TX 77522-0431
409-762-9334

Iris & Plus
595 River St.
Cowansville, PQ J2K 3G6
Canada
450-266-0181
Fax: 450-266-0181

Isabel Hibbard Gardens
4 Nancy Dr.
South Farmingdale, NY 11735
516-694-9682

Isokern Fireplaces/Earthcore Industries
8917 Western Way
Ste. 120
Jacksonville, FL 32256
904-363-3417
1-800-642-2920
Fax: 904-363-3408
www.isokeruk.com

J & L Orchids
20 Sherwood Rd.
Easton, CT 06612
203-261-3772
Fax: 203-261-8730
www.orchidmall.com/jlorchids

JA Nearing Co.
9390 Davis Ave.
Laurel, MD 20723
301-498-5700
1-800-323-6933
Fax: 301-497-9751

Jacuzzi Whirlpool Bath
P.O. Drawer J
2121 N. California Blvd.
Ste. 475
Walnut Creek, CA 94596
925-938-7070
1-800-288-4002
Fax: 925-938-3025
www.jacuzzi.com

Jamo
8850 N.W. 79th Ave.
Miami, FL 33166
305-885-3444
1-800-826-6852
Fax: 305-883-5591
www.jamoinc.com

Jancik Arts
2630 S.W. 87th Pl.
Ocala, FL 34476
352-237-1593
Fax: 404-892-3887
www.jancikarts.com

Jerry Horne Rare Plants
10195 S.W. 70th St.
Miami, FL 33173
305-270-1235

JKR Design/Build
341 Schwartz Rd.
Gettysburg, PA 17325-8622
717-338-0157
717-338-0247
E-mail:builderken@cvn.net

J.L. Matthews Co.
620 W. Felix St.
Fort Worth, TX 76115-3403
817-924-3360
1-800-421-3360
Fax: 817-923-0246
www.jlmatthews.com

John Deere
Worldwide Commercial & Consumer Equip. Div.
P.O. Box 29533
Raleigh, NC 27626
1-800-537-8233
www.deere.com

John Gordon Nursery
1385 Campbell Blvd.
Amherst, NY 14228
716-691-9371

Johnny's Selected Seeds
Foss Hill Rd., Box 2580
Albion, ME 04910
207-437-9294
Fax: 207-437-2165
www.johnnyseeds.com

Johnson Daylily Garden
70 Lark Ave.
Brooksville, FL 34601-1319
352-544-0330
E-mail:gjohnson@atlantic.net

Johnson Nursery
5273 Hwy. 52E
Ellijay, GA 30540
706-276-3187
1-888-276-3187
Fax: 706-276-3186
www.johnsonnursery.com

Jomoco Products Co.
9999 E. 59th St.
Tulsa, OK 74146-6408
918-252-3000
1-800-322-5277
Fax: 918-252-4444
www.jomocoproducts.com

Joyce Mfg.
5400 W. 161 St.
Cleveland, OH 44142
216-433-4343
1-800-824-7988
Fax: 216-433-0558
Only in Midwest, South, East

Justice Design Group
11244 Playa Ct.
Culver City, CA 90230
310-397-8300
Fax: 310-397-7170
www.jdg.com

Kadco USA
P.O. Box 584
Amsterdam, NY 12010

Karl Kuemmerling, Inc.
129 Edgewater Ave. N.W.
Massillon, OH 44646-3396
330-477-3457
1-888-222-6166
1-800-464-8227
Fax: 330-477-8528
E-mail:kuemmerling@ezo.net

Karnak Corp.
330 Central Ave.
Clark, NJ 07066
732-388-0300
1-800-526-4236
Fax: 732-388-9422

Kasch Nursery
2860 NE Kelly Pl.
Gresham, OR 97030
503-661-0357

Kay's Greenhouses
207 W. Southcross
San Antonio, TX 78221-1155

KCI Coatings
201 E. Market
P.O. Box 1093
Louisville, KY 40202
502-584-0151
Fax: 502-584-1601

Kester's Wild Game Food Nurseries
P.O. Box 516
Omro, WI 54963
920-685-2929
1-800-558-8815
Fax: 920-685-6727
www.kestersnursery.com

Keystone Retaining Wall Systems
444 W. 78th St.
Minneapolis, MN 55435
612-897-1040
1-800-891-9791
Fax: 612-897-3858
www.keystonewalls.com

Kichler Lighting
7711 E. Pleasant Valley Rd.
Independence, OH 44131
216-573-1000
Fax: 216-573-1001

Kinsman Co.
River Rd.
Point Pleasant, PA 18950

Kirkland Daylilies
P.O. Box 176
Newville, AL 36353
334-889-3313

Klean-Strip
P.O. Box 1879
Memphis, TN 38101
901-775-0100
1-800-238-2672
Fax: 800-621-9508

Kodiak
P.O. Box 9158
416 E. Brooks Rd.
Memphis, TN 38109
901-344-5350
1-800-K-KODIAK
Fax: 901-344-5387
www.kodiakwood.com

Kraft Tool Co.
8325 Hedge Lane Ter.
Shawnee, KS 66227
913-422-4848
Fax: 913-422-1018

Kramer Equipment
7835 Richmond Hwy.
Alexandria, VA 22306-7897
703-360-4777

Kroy Building Products
P.O. Box 636
2719 Division Ave.
York, NE 68467
402-362-1212
1-800-933-5769
Fax: 402-362-6797
www.kroybp.com

KSA Jojoba
19025 Partenia St.
Northridge, CA 91324
818-701-1534
Fax: 818-993-0194
E-mail:jojoba99@hotmail.com/

Kuk's Forest Nursery
10174 Barr Rd.
Brecksville, OH 44141-3302
440-546-2675
Fax: 440-546-2675

Kuny's Mfg. Co.
5901 44A St.
Leduc, AB T9E 7B8
Canada
403-986-1151
Fax: 403-986-9861

Kunz Engineering
242 N. 45th Rd., RR 1
Mendota, IL 61342-9413

815-539-6954
Fax: 815-539-6954

L & L Nursery Supply
5350 G St.
Chino, CA 91710-5215
909-591-0461
1-800-624-2517
Fax: 909-591-3280
E-mail:info@llsupply.attmail.com

Ladybug Daylilies
1852 E. SR 46
Geneva, FL 32732-7248
407-349-0271
Fax: 407-349-2688
E-mail:ladybug@magicnet.net

Landscape Structures
601 7th St. South
Delano, MN 55328
612-972-3391
1-800-328-0035
Fax: 612-973-3185
www.playlsi.com

Larner Seeds
P.O. Box 407
Bolinas, CA 94924
415-868-9407
Fax: 415-868-9820

Larry W. Price Books
353 N.W. Maywood Dr.
Portland, OR 97210
503-221-1410
E-mail:lwprice@gateway.net

Laticrete Intl.
1 Laticrete Park N.
Bethany, CT 06524
203-393-0010
1-800-243-4788
Fax: 203-393-1684
www.laticrete.com

L.B. Plastics
482 E. Plaza Dr.
P.O. Box 907
Mooresville, NC 28115
704-663-1543
1-800-752-7739
Fax: 704-664-2989

Lee Gardens
P.O. Box 5
Tremont, IL 61568
309-925-5262
Fax: 309-925-5010
E-mail:jiboshi@aol.com

Lee Valley Tools
P.O. Box 6295, Station J
Ottawa, ON K2A 1T4
Canada

1-800-267-8767
Fax: 800-668-1807
www.leevalley.com

Lee's Botanical Garden
P.O. Box 669
LaBelle, FL 33975-0669
941-675-8728

Legacy Timber Frames
691 County Rd. 70
Stillwater, NY 12170
518-279-9108
Fax: 518-581-9219

Leslie-Locke
4501 Circle 75 Pkwy.
Ste. F 6300
Atlanta, GA 30339
770-953-6366
1-800-755-9392
Fax: 770-956-0663

Lewis Mountain Herbs & Everlastings
2345 State Rt. 247
Manchester, OH 45144
937-549-2484
1-800-71-HERBS
Fax: 937-549-2886
E-mail:mtherbs@bright.net

Liberty Seed Co.
P.O. Box 806
461 Robinson Dr. S.E.
New Philadelphia, OH \ 44663
330-364-1611
1-800-541-6022
Fax: 330-364-6415
www.libertyseed.com

Lighting by Hammerworks
P.O. Box 945
118 Main St.
Meredith, NH 03253
603-279-7352
Fax: 603-279-7352 ext. 51
www.hammerworks.com

Lightolier
631 Airport Rd.
Fall River, MA 02720
508-679-8131
1-800-215-1068
Fax: 508-646-3204
www.lightolier.com

Lightway Industries
28435 Industry Dr.
Valencia, CA 91355
805-257-0286
1-800-325-4448
Fax: 805-257-0201
www.lightwayind.com

Lily of the Valley Herb Farm
3969 Fox Ave.
Minerva, OH 44657
330-862-3920
Fax: 330-862-9013
Only in Midwest, South, East

Limerock Ornamental Grasses
70 Sawmill Rd.
Port Matilda, PA 16870
814-692-2272
Fax: 814-692-9848
E-mail:limerock@juno.com

Lindal Cedar Homes/Sunrooms
4300 S. 104th Pl.
Seattle, WA 98178
206-725-0900
1-800-426-0536
Fax: 206-725-1615
www.lindal.com

Linden House Gardening Books
148 Sylvan Ave.
Scarborough, ON
M1M 1K4 Canada
416-269-0699
Fax: 416-269-0615
www.icangarden.com/linden.htm

Lister's Sod Farm
P.O. Box 127
Wewahitchka, FL
32465-0127
850-639-2728
Only in South

Liteway
P.O. Box 700
1119 Beaver St.
Bristol, PA 19007
215-788-5585
Fax: 215-788-5057

Little Beaver Inc.
P.O. Box 840
Livingston, TX
77351-0840
409-327-3121
Fax: 409-327-4025
www.littlebeaver.com

Little Wonder
1028 Street Rd.
Southampton, PA
18966-4217
215-357-5111
1-877-596-6337
www.littlewonder.com

Little's Good Gloves
P.O. Box 808
Johnstown, NY 12095
518-762-3312
1-888-967-5548
Fax: 518-762-2980

Living Stones Nursery
2936 N. Stone Ave.
Tucson, AZ 85705
520-628-8773
Fax: 520-628-8773
www.lithops.net

L.M. Scofield Co.
6533 Bandini Blvd.
Los Angeles, CA 90040
213-720-3000
1-800-800-9900
Fax: 213-720-3030

Lon J. Rombough
P.O. Box 365
Aurora, OR 97002-0365
503-678-1410
www.hevanet.com/
lonrom

London Tile Co.
65 Walnut St.
New London, OH 44851
419-929-1551
Fax: 419-929-1552

Lowen Sign Co.
1330 E. Fourth St.
P.O. Box 1528
Hutchinson, KS
67504-1528
316-663-2161
1-800-545-5505
Fax: 800-846-4466

Ludwig Industries
133 Middleton St.
Brooklyn, NY 11206
718-387-0947
1-800-827-2312
Fax: 718-387-0824

MAAX
Div. Acrylica, Premium
600 Rt. Cameron
Ste-Marie, PQ G6E 1B2
Canada
418-387-4155
1-800-463-6229
Fax: 418-387-3507
www.maax.com

Macco
925 Euclid Ave.
Cleveland, OH 44115
216-334-8000
1-800-634-0015
Fax: 216-344-7319
www.liquidnails.com

MacKissic
Box 111
Parker Ford, PA
19457-0111
610-495-7181
Fax: 610-495-5951
E-mail:mackissic1@msn.
com

Macklanburg-Duncan
4041 N. Santa Fe
Oklahoma City, OK 73118
405-528-4411
1-800-654-8454
Fax: 405-557-3668
www.macdunc.com

Magic Circle Corp.
6302 E. County
   Road 100 N.
Coatesville, IN
46121-9609
765-246-6845
1-800-233-7596
Fax: 765-246-6146
www.dixiechopper.com

Maine Millstones
P.O. Box 228
Southport, ME 04576
207-633-6091
Fax: 207-633-6095

**Mainline of North
America**
81 US Rt. 40
London, OH 43140
740-852-9733
1-800-837-2097
Fax: 740-852-2045

Mainline Tillers
81 US Rt. 40
London, OH 43140
740-852-9733
1-800-837-2097
Fax: 740-852-2045
E-mail:
theresamainline@
hotmail.com

**Mansfield Plumbing
Products**
8425 Pulsar Pl., Ste. 220
Columbus, OH 43240
614-825-0960
Fax: 614-825-0989

Mantis
1028 Street Rd.
Southhampton, PA 18966
1-800-366-6268
Fax: 215-364-1409
www.mantisgardentools.
com

Marathon Spa & Bath
1549 Hwy. 36 N.
Rosenberg, TX 77471
281-342-8775
Fax: 281-342-8756

Marell Industries
453 Hwy. 74 S.
Peachtree City, GA
30269-2001
770-487-0481
1-800-864-4510
Fax: 770-487-5494

Marketshare
2001 Tarob Ct.
Milpitas, CA 95035
408-934-8301
Fax: 408-262-9328

Martin-Senour
101 Prospect Ave., N.W.
Cleveland, OH 44115
1-800-677-5270
Fax: 216-566-1655

The Marugg Co.
P.O. Box 1418
Tracy City, TN 37387
931-592-5042
Fax: 931-924-2705
E-mail:jbaggenstoss@
infoave.net

Mary's Plant Farm
2410 Lanes Mill Rd.
Hamilton, OH 45013
513-894-0022
Fax: 513-892-2053

Masco Corp.
21001 Van Born Rd.
Taylor, MI 48180
313-274-7400
Fax: 313-792-6666
www.masco.com

Mason Corp.
P.O. Box 59226
Birmingham, AL
35259-9226
205-942-4100
1-800-868-4100
Fax: 205-945-4399

Masters Choice
200 Harrison St.
P.O. Box 938
Jamestown, NY 14702
716-487-0007
1-800-624-6434

McCulloch Corp.
P.O. Box 11990
Tucson, AZ 85734-1990
520-574-1311

McGrevor Coatings
1701 Utica Ave.
Brooklyn, NY 11234
718-377-0505
1-800-922-9981
Fax: 718-253-4430

Mel Northey Co.
303 Gulf Bank Rd.
Houston, TX 77037
281-445-3485
1-800-828-0302
Fax: 281-445-7456
www.melnorthey.com

Mellco
P.O. Drawer C
Perry, GA 31069
1-800-866-1414
Fax: 800-777-3299
www.melco.com

Melnor, Inc.
P.O. Box 2840, 3085
Shawnee Dr.
Winchester, VA
22604-2040
540-722-5600
1-888-411-2500
Fax: 540-722-1131
www.melnor.com

**Mendocino Heirloom
Roses**
P.O. Box 670
Mendocino, CA 95460
707-937-0963
Fax: 707-937-3744
E-mail:gdaly@mcn.org

Miami Water Lilies
22150 S.W. 147th Ave.
Miami, FL 33170
305-258-2664
Fax: 305-258-1151

**Mid-America Building
Products Corp.**
A Tapco Intl. Corp.
45657 Port St.
Plymouth, MI 48170-6010
313-459-5151
1-800-521-8486
Fax: 313-459-3647
www.tapco-intl.com

Mid-America Gardens
P.O. Box 18278
Salem, OR 97305-8278
503-390-6072
Fax: 503-390-6072

Midwest Cactus
P.O. Box 163
New Melle, MO 63365
314-828-5389
E-mail:csmith01@mail.
win.org

Midwest Wildflowers
Box 64
Rockton, IL 61072
www.home1.gte.net/
busker/index.htm

Minwax Co.
10 Mountainview Rd.
Upper Saddle River, NJ
07458
201-391-0253
1-800-526-0495
Fax: 201-573-9022

**Miracle Sealants &
Abrasives**
12806 Schabarum Ave.
Bldg. A
Irwindale, CA 91706
626-814-8988
1-800-350-1901
Fax: 626-851-8932
www.miraclesealants.com

MN Productions
P.O. Box 577
Freeland, WA 98249-0577
360-331-7995
Fax: 360-341-6208
E-mail:mnpro@whidbey.
com

**Moon Mountain
Wildflowers**
P.O. Box 725
Carpinteria, CA
93014-0725
805-684-2565
Fax: 805-684-2798
E-mail:ssseeds@silcom.
com

Morco Products
P.O. Box 160
Dundas, MN 55019
507-645-4277

Morlite Systems
321 Mechanic St.
Girard, PA 16417
814-774-9631
Fax: 814-774-2345

**Mother Nature's
Worm Castings**
Box 1055
Avon, CT 06001
860-673-3029
Fax: 860-673-3029
www.homeharvest.com

Moultrie Mfg.
P.O. Box 2948
Moultrie, GA 31776-2948
912-985-1312
1-800-841-8674
Fax: 912-890-7246
www.moultriemfgco.com

**Mountain Valley
Growers**
38325 Pepperweed Rd.
Squaw Valley, CA 93675
209-338-2775
Fax: 209-338-0075
www.
mountainvalleygrowers.
com

**MTC (Media Trade
Corp.)**
11641 Red Hibiscus Dr.
Bonita Springs, FL 34135
941-948-2001
Fax: 941-948-2002
E-mail:gginsberg@
compuserve.com

MTD Pro
P.O. Box 368022
Cleveland, OH
44136-9722
877-MTD-PRO1
www.mtdproducts.com

**Multi-Seal Pacific
Corp.**
1109 S. Fremont Ave.
Alhambra, CA 91803
626-282-5659
1-800-222-6915
Fax: 626-282-8516

Muralo Co.
148 E. Fifth St.
Bayonne, NJ 07002
201-437-0770
1-800-631-3440
Fax: 201-437-2316
Only in Midwest, South, East

Mushroompeople
P.O. Box 220
Summertown, TN 38483-
2200
931-964-2200
1-800-692-6329
Fax: 800-386-4496
www.thefarm.org/
mushroom

**National Concrete
Masonry Assn.**
2302 Horse Pen Rd.
Herndon, VA 20171-3499
703-713-1900
Fax: 703-713-1910
www.ncma.org

**National Paint and
Coatings Assn.**
1500 Rhode Island Ave.,
N.W.
Washington, DC
20005-5503
202-462-6272
Fax: 202-462-0347
www.paint.org

**National Spa and Pool
Institute**
2111 Eisenhower Ave.
Alexandria, VA
22314-4698
703-838-0083
Fax: 703-549-0493
www.resourcecenter.com

Native Gardens
5737 Fisher Ln.
Greenback, TN 37742
423-856-0220
Fax: 423-856-0220

Native Seeds
14590 Triadelphia Mill Rd.
Dayton, MD 21036
301-596-9818
Fax: 301-854-3195
E-mail:saund10449@aol.
com

Nature's Control
P.O. Box 35
Medford, OR 97501
541-899-8318
Fax: 800-698-6250
E-mail:
bugnc@teleport.com

Nature's Garden
40611 Hwy. 226
Scio, OR 97374
503-394-3217

NDS
851 N. Harvard Ave.
Lindsay, CA 93247
209-562-9888
1-800-726-1994
Fax: 800-726-1998
www.ndspro.com

Necessary Organics
One Nature's Way
P.O. Box 305
New Castle, VA 24127
1-800-447-5354
Fax: 540-864-5186
www.concerngarden.com

Nedia Enterprises
89-66 217th St.
Jamaica, NY 11427
718-740-5171
1-888-725-6999
Fax: 718-740-1049
www.nedia.com

Neenah Foundry Co.
2121 Brooks Ave
P.O. Box 729
Neenah, WI 54957
920-725-7000
Fax: 920-729-3661
E-mail:constsales@nfco.
com

Nessen Lighting
420 Railroad Way
Mamaroneck, NY 10543
914-698-7799
Fax: 914-698-5577

**New England Wild
Flower Society**
180 Hemenway Rd.
Framingham, MA 01701
508-877-7630
www.newfs.org/~newfs/

**Newstamp
Lighting Co.**
227 Bay Rd.
P.O. Box 189
North Easton, MA 02356
508-238-7071
Fax: 508-230-8312

**Newtown Power
Equipment**
151 Mount Pleasant Rd.
Newtown, CT 06470-1438
203-426-5012

Nitron Industries
P.O. Box 1447
Fayetteville, AR 72702
501-587-1777
1-800-835-0123
Fax: 501-587-0177
www.nitron.com

Nixalite of America
P.O. Box 727
1025 16th Ave.
East Moline, IL 61244
309-755-8771
1-800-624-1189
Fax: 800-624-1196
www.nixalite.com

**Northeastern
Associates**
19 Commerce RD No. H
Fairfield, NJ 07004-1630
973-227-0359
1-800-261-7772

**Northern Greenhouse
Sales**
P.O. Box 42LG
Neche, ND 58265
204-327-5540
Fax: 204-327-5527

**Northern Kiwi
Nursery**
RR 3, 181 Niven Rd.
Niagara-on-the-Lake, ON
L0S 1J0 Canada
905-937-2031
www.niagara.com/
~pklassen

Northern Paint Canada
394 Gertrude Ave.
P.O. Box 3030
Winnipeg, MB R3C 4E5
Canada
204-958-5400
Fax: 204-453-6731

The Northern Roof Tile Sales Co.
4408 Milestrip Rd.
Ste. 266
Blasdell, NY 14219
905-627-4035
Fax: 905-627-9648
www.wchat.on.ca/
commercial/nrts

Northplan/ Mountain Seed
P.O. Box 9107
Moscow, ID 83843
208-882-8040
Fax: 208-882-7446
E-mail:norplan@moscow.
com

Northridge Gardens
9821 White Oak Ave.
Northridge, CA 91325
818-349-9798
Fax: 818-349-9798
E-mail:
norgardens@aol.com

Northwind Nursery and Orchards
7910 335th Ave. N.W.
Princeton, MN 55371
612-389-4920
E-mail:northwind9@juno.
com

Norway Co.
E9237 County Road O
Sauk City, WI 53583-9660
608-544-5000

Nourse Farms
41 River Rd.
South Deerfield, MA
    01373
413-665-2658
Fax: 413-665-7888
www.noursefarms.com

Nuccio's Nurseries
P.O. Box 6160
Altadena, CA 91003
626-794-3383

Nurseries at North Glen
Rt. 2, Box 2700
Glen St. Mary, FL 32040
904-259-2754
E-mail:palmdoctor@aol.
com

Oakes Daylilies
8204 Monday Rd.
Corryton, TN 37721
423-687-3770
1-800-532-9545
Fax: 423-688-8186
www.oakesdaylilies.com

Oakridge Nursery
P.O. Box 182
East Kingston, NH 03827
603-642-7339
Fax: 603-642-6827

The October Co.
P.O. Box 71, 51 Ferry St.
Easthampton, MA 01027
413-527-9380
1-800-628-9346
Fax: 413-527-0091

Ohio Earth Food
5488 Swamp St. N.E.
Hartville, OH 44632
330-877-9356
Fax: 330-877-4237

Olallie Daylilies Gardens
129 Auger Hole Rd.
South Newfane, VT
05351-7901
802-348-6614
Fax: 802-348-9881
www.sover.net/~darrowcs

Old Carolina Brick Co.
475 Majolica Rd.
Salisbury, NC 28147
704-636-8850
Fax: 704-636-0000

Old House Gardens
536 Third St.
Ann Arbor, MI 48103
734-995-1486
Fax: 734-995-1687
www.oldhousegardens.
com

Old Masters
1900 Albany Pl. S.
Orange City, IA 51041
712-737-3436
1-800-747-3436
Fax: 712-737-3893

Old Strathcona Garden Shoppe
10820-82 Ave.
Edmonton, AL T6E 2B3
Canada
780-434-7401
Fax: 780-434-7401
www.icangarden.com

Olson Irrigations Systems
P.O. Box 711570
Santee, CA 92072-1570
619-562-3100
Fax: 619-562-2724
E-mail:h2olson@pacbell.
net

Olympic Paints and Stains
1 PPG Place
Pittsburgh, PA 15272
412-434-3131
1-800-235-5020

Omega Sunspaces
3852 Hawkins N.W.
Albuquerque, NM 87109
505-344-0333
1-800-753-3034
Fax: 505-344-0641

Oregon Research & Development Corp.
Snow Roof Systems
1895 16th St. S.E.
Salem, OR 97302-1436
503-588-7000
1-800-345-0809
Fax: 800-588-2075
www.cyberhighway.
net/~snowroof

Oregon Trail Daffodils
41905 S. E. Louden
Corbett, OR 97019
503-695-5513
Fax: 503-695-5573
E-mail:daffodil@europa.
com

The Original Bug Shirt Co.
908 Niagara Falls Blvd.
Suite 467
North Tonawanda, NY
14120-2063
705-729-5620
1-800-998-9096
Fax: 705-729-5625
www.bugshirt.com

Osmose Wood Preserving
1016 Everee Inn Rd.
Griffin, GA 30223
770-228-8434
1-800-686-6676
Fax: 770-229-5225
www.osmose.com

Osram Sylvania
100 Endicott St.
Danvers, MA 01923
508-777-1900
1-800-544-4828
Fax: 508-750-2152

Out of the Redwoods
P.O. Box 1972
Clackamas, OR 97015
503-658-4135

P & P Seed Co.
14050 Rt. 62
Collins, NY 14034-9704
716-532-5995
1-800-449-5681
Fax: 716-532-5690
E-mail:lgourd@aol.com

Pacific Clay Brick Products
P.O. Box 549
Lake Elsinore, CA
92531-0549
909-674-2131
Fax: 909-674-4909

Pacific Tree Farms
4301 Lynwood Dr.
Chula Vista, CA
91910-3226
619-422-2400
Fax: 619-426-6759

Package Pavement Co.
Rt. 52
P.O. Box 408
Stormville, NY
12582-0408
914-221-2224
1-800-724-8193
Fax: 914-221-0433

Palmer Industries
10611 Old Annapolis Rd.
Frederick, MD
21701-3347
301-898-7848
Fax: 301-898-3312

Pampered Plant Nursery
P.O. Box 3
Bourbonnais, IL
60914-0003
815-937-6949
E-mail:nurseryplantsppn@
technologist.com

Panasonic
1 Panasonic Way, 4A-4
Secaucus, NJ 07094
201-392-6442
1-800-553-0384
Fax: 201-348-7003

Paradise Water Gardens
14 May St.
Whitman, MA 02382
781-447-4711
Fax: 781-447-4591
E-mail:pstet82982@aol.
com

Parex
P.O. Box 189
Redan, GA 30074
770-482-7872
1-800-LE PAREX
Fax: 770-482-6878
www.parex.com

Park Place
2251 Wisconsin Ave. N.W.
Washington, DC 20007
202-342-6294
202-342-9255

Parker Sweeper
111 S. Rohlwing Rd.
Addison, IL 60101-3027
630-627-6900
630-627-1130

Parks Corp.
1 West St.
Fall River, MA 02720
508-679-5938
1-800-225-8543
Fax: 508-674-8404

Patio Garden Ponds
2500 N. Moore Ave
Moore, OK 73160
405-793-7661
1-800-487-5459
Fax: 405-793-9669
www.
patio-garden-ponds.com

The Patriot Co.
944 N. 45th St.
Milwaukee, WI 53208
414-259-8997
1-800-798-2447
Fax: 414-259-9612
www.patriot-company.
com

Pave Tech
P.O. Box 576
Prior Lake, MN 55372
612-226-4600
1-800-728-3832
Fax: 612-226-4606
www.pavetech.com

Paveloc Industries
8302 S. Rt. 23
Marengo, IL 60152
815-568-4700
1-800-590-2772
Fax: 815-568-1210
Only in Midwest

**Paw Paw Everlast
Label Co.**
P.O. Box 93
Paw Paw, MI 49079

**Penofin-Performance
Coatings**
P.O. Box 1569, 360 Lake
Mendocino Dr.
Ukiah, CA 95482
707-462-3023
1-800-PENOFIN
Fax: 707-462-6139
www.penofin.com

Pense Nursery
Rt. 2, Box 330-A
Mountainburg, AR 72946
501-369-2494
Fax: 501-369-2494
www.alcasoft.com/pense

The Pepper Gal
P.O. Box 23006
Ft. Lauderdale, FL 33307
954-537-5540
Fax: 954-566-2208

Perky-Pet Products
2201 S. Wabash St.
Denver, CO 80231-3313
303-751-9000
Fax: 303-368-9616
www.perky-pet.com

Perlite of Texas
14040 Judson Rd.
San Antonio, TX
78233-4420
210-653-1635

Permalatt
P.O. Box 853
Lexington, NE
68850-0853
308-324-2227
1-888-457-4342
Fax: 308-324-2381

Peter Pauls Nurseries
4665 Chapin Rd.
Canadaigua, NY 14424
716-394-7397
Fax: 716-394-4122
www.peterpauls.com

Petmal Supply Co.
830 Atlantic Ave.
Baldwin, NY 11510
516-867-4573
Fax: 516-867-4691

Philips Lighting Co.
200 Franklin Square Dr.
Somerset, NJ 08875
908-563-3215
Fax: 908-563-3641
www.philips.com/lighting/

Philstone Fasteners
11 Cove St.
P.O. Box 41389
New Bedford, MA
02744-1389
508-990-2054
1-800-225-9015
Fax: 508-984-5547

Pineapple Place
3961 Markharm Woods
Rd.
Longwood, FL 32779
407-333-0445
Fax: 407-829-6616

**Pinecliffe Daylily
Gardens**
6604 Scottsville Rd.
Floyds Knob, IN 47119
812-923-8113
Fax: 812-923-9618
www.gardeneureka.com/
pine

Pinetree Garden Seeds
Box 300, 616A Lewiston
Rd.
New Gloucester, ME
04260
207-926-3400
Fax: 888-52-SEEDS
Fax: 207-926-3886
(outside U.S.)
www.superseeds.com

**PL Adhesives &
Sealants**
ChemRex
889 Valley Park Dr.
Shakopee, MN 55379
612-496-6000
1-800-433-9517
Fax: 612-496-6062

P.L. Rohrer & Bro.
P.O. Box 250
Smoketown, PA 17576
717-299-2571
Fax: 800-468-4944
E-mail: pl-rohrer@
compuserve.com

Planet Natural
1512 Gold Ave.
Bozeman, MT 59715
406-587-5891
Fax: 406-587-0223
www.planetnatural.com

**Plantasia Cactus
Gardens**
867 Filer Ave. West
Twin Falls, ID 83301
208-734-7959
E-mail:lorton@
computer-depot.com

**Plant Delights
Nursery**
9241 Sauls Rd.
Raleigh, NC 27603
919-772-4794
Fax: 919-662-0370
www.plantdel.com

Plants of the Wild
P.O. Box 866
Tekoa, WA 99033
509-284-2848
Fax: 509-284-6464
www.plantsofthewild.com

**Plastics Research
Corp.**
3200 Robert T. Longway
Flint, MI 48506
810-235-0400
1-800-879-7723
Fax: 810-235-0401

Plastival
3050 Boul, Industriel
Chomedey, Laval, PQ
H7L 4P7 Canada
514-629-5050
Fax: 514-629-5052

**Plumbing
Manufacturers
Institute**
800 Roosevelt Rd.
Bldg. C, Ste. 20
Glen Ellyn, IL 60137-5833
708-858-9172
Fax: 708-790-3095

Point Electric
P.O. Box 619
Nanuet, NY 10954-0619
914-623-3471
Fax: 914-623-1861
E-mail:swivelier@juno.
com

Poly-Wall Intl.
8400 Coral Sea St., N.E
Ste. 800
Blaine, MN 55449
612-780-0161
1-800-846-3020
Fax: 612-780-0170
www.poly-wall.com

Pompeian Studios
90 Rockledge Rd.
Bronxville, NY
10708-5208
914-337-5595
1-800-457-5595
Fax: 914-337-5661
E-mail:pamhumbert@
worldnet.att.net

Poston Equipment Sales
1430 O'Day Rd.
Pearland, TX 77581-7224
281-997-7500
1-800-243-6008
Fax: 281-997-7822

PPG Industries
1 PPG Pl.
Pittsburgh, PA 15272
412-434-3131
1-800-2-GETPPG (Glass)
1-800-441-9695 (Paint)
Fax: 412-434-2821

Prairie Moon Nursery
Rt. 2, Box 163
Winona, MN 55987-9515
507-452-1362
Fax: 507-454-5238
E-mail:pmnrsy@hbci.com

Prairie Ridge Nursery/CRM Ecosystems, Inc.
9738 Overland Rd.
Mt. Horeb, WI 53572
608-437-5245
Fax: 608-437-8982
E-mail:crmprairie@
inxpress.com

Pratt & Lambert
75 Tonawanda St.
Buffalo, NY 14207
716-873-6000
Fax: 716-877-9646

Pratt's Power Equipment
5241 W. Glendale Ave.
Glendale, AZ 85301-2603
602-939-3326
Fax: 602-939-1732

Precision Multiple Controls
33 Greenwood Ave.
Midland Park, NJ 07432
201-444-0600
Fax: 201-444-8575
E-mail:precisionmultiple@
worldnet.att.net

Premier Environmental Products
P.O. Box 218469
Houston, TX 77218-8469
281-893-8088
1-800-829-0215
Fax: 409-885-7959

Premier Wood Floors
(A Div. of Triangle Pacific Corp.)
16803 Dallas Pkwy.

Dallas, TX 75248-6196
214-887-2050
1-800-722-4647
Fax: 214-887-2234
www.trianglepacific.com

Prentiss Court Ground Covers
P.O. Box 8662
Greenville, SC 29604
864-277-4037
Fax: 864-299-5015

Prescolite-Moldcast
1251 Doolittle Dr.
San Leandro, CA 94577
510-562-3500
Fax: 510-577-5022

Pro Lawn Equipment
4225 Pro St.
Shreveport, LA
71109-6406
318-635-8184
1-800-282-8768
Fax: 318-635-9679
www.promowers.com

Progress Lighting
P.O. Box 5704
Spartanburg, SC
29304-5704
864-599-6000
Fax: 864-599-6151

ProSoCo.
P.O. Box 171677
Kansas City, KS 66117
913-281-2700
1-800-255-4255
Fax: 913-281-4385

Prudential Building Materials
171 Milton St.
East Dedham, MA 02026
617-329-3232
1-800-444-9585
Fax: 617-326-0752
Only in South, East

PS Aluminum Products
8055 Marco-Polo Ave.
Montreal, PQ H1E 5Y8
Canada
514-648-1100
Fax: 514-648-9335
Only in South, East

Quality Lighting
11530 Melrose Ave.
Franklin Park, IL 60131
847-451-0040
Fax: 847-451-6768

Quality Systems
501 Metroplex Dr.

Ste. 115
Nashville, TN 37211-3127
615-331-9200
1-800-607-3762
Fax: 615-834-1335
www.permacrete.com

Quarry Tile Co.
6328 Utah Ave.
Spokane, WA 99212
509-536-2812
1-800-423-2608
Fax: 509-536-4072

Quick Crete Products Corp.
P.O. Box 639
Norco, CA 91760
909-737-6240
Fax: 909-737-7032

The Quikrete Cos.
2987 Clairmont Rd.
Ste. 500
Atlanta, GA 30329
404-634-9100
Fax: 404-634-9568

Quinstar Corp.
P.O. Box 424
Quinter, KS 67752-0424
785-754-3355
Fax: 785-754-2491

R & R Products
3334 E. Milber St.
Tucson, AZ 85714-2097
520-889-2592
1-800-528-3446
Fax: 520-294-1045
www.rrproducts.com

RAB Electric Mfg. Co.
170 Ludlow Ave.
Northvale, NJ 07647
201-784-8600
1-800-938-1010
Fax: 201-784-0077
www.rabweb.com

Rahn Trellis Co.
(A Div. of MHJ Group)
4290 Alatex Rd.
Montgomery, AL 36108
334-281-0097
1-800-260-8993
Fax: 334-281-0575

Rainbow Roof Systems by Madden Mfg.
1889 N.W. 22nd St.
Pompano Beach, FL 33069
1-800-272-2071
Fax: 305-960-0567

Rasland Farm
NC 82 at US 13
Godwin, NC 28344
910-567-2705
Fax: 910-567-6716
www.alcasoft.com/
rasland/

Raylux
P.O. Box 619
Nanuet, NY 10954-0619
914-623-3471
Fax: 914-623-1861
E-mail:raylux@juno.com

Raymond M. Sutton, Jr. Books
430 Main St.
Williamsburg, KY
40769-0330
606-549-3464
Fax: 606-549-3469
www.suttonbooks.com

Redland Brick (Cushwa Plant)
P.O. Box 160
Williamsport, MD 21795
1-800-366-2742
Fax: 301-223-6675
www.redlandbrick.com

Red's Rhodies
15920 S.W. Oberst Ln.
Sherwood, OR 97140
503-625-6331
E-mail:rhodies@pcez.com

Reemay
P.O. Box 511
70 Old Hickory Blvd.
Old Hickory, TN 37138
615-847-7000
1-800-321-6271
Fax: 615-847-7068
www.reemay.com

Regent Lighting Corp.
2611 La Vista Dr.
P.O. Box 2658
Burlington, NC 27216
919-226-2411
1-800-334-6871
Fax: 919-222-5158
www.regentlighting.com

Reinco
520 North Ave.
P.O. Box 512
Plainfield, NJ 07061-0512
908-755-0921
1-800-526-7687
Fax: 908-755-6379
www.reinco.com

The Reinforced Earth Co.
8614 Westwood Center

Dr., Ste. 1100
Vienna, VA 22182
703-821-1175
1-800-446-5700
Fax: 703-821-1815
www.recousa.com

**Rejuvenation Lamp &
Fixture Co.**
1100 S.E. Grand Ave.
Portland, OR 97214
503-231-1900
1-888-343-8548
1-888-401-1900
Fax: 800-526-7329
www.rejuvenation.com

Renato Bisazza
8032 N.W. 66th St.
Miami, FL 33166-2728
305-597-4099
E-mail:laura@bisazzausa.
com

**Reo Temp
Instrument Corp.**
11568 Sorrento Valley Rd.
Suite 10
San Diego, CA 92121
619-481-7737
1-800-648-7737
Fax: 619-481-7150
www.reotemp.com

**ReSource Building
Products**
920 Davis Rd., Ste. 101
Elgin, IL 60123
847-931-4771
1-800-231-9721

**Resource
Conservation
Technology**
2633 N. Calvert St.
Baltimore, MD
21218-4617
410-366-1146
1-800-477-7724
Fax: 410-366-1202

The Reveg Edge
P.O. Box 609
Redwood City, CA 94064
650-325-7333
Fax: 650-325-4056
www.batnet.com/
rwc-seed/reveg.html

Reynolds Metals Co.
(Construction Products
Div.)
6601 W. Broad St.
P.O. Box 27003
Richmond, VA 23230
804-281-2000
Fax: 804-281-3602

Rio Plastics
P.O. Box 3707
Brownsville, TX 78523
956-831-2715
Fax: 956-831-9851

Risi Stone Systems
8500 Leslie St., Suite 390
Thornhill, ON L3T 7M8
Canada
905-882-5898
1-800-626-9255
Fax: 905-882-4556
www.risistone.com

Riverdale Iris Gardens
4652 Culver Ave. N.W.
Buffalo, MN 55313
320-963-6810

R.J. Winmore
P.O. Box 1765
Sioux Falls, SD
57101-1765
605-332-0223
Fax: 605-335-8595

**RK Mfg. Grassye
Pavers**
P.O. Box 1739
Ridgeland, MS
39158-1739
601-957-5575
1-800-957-5575
Fax: 601-957-5577
www.rkmrg.com

Robert Compton, Ltd.
RD 3, Box 3600
Bristol, VT 05443

**Roberts Step-Lite
Systems**
8413 Mantle Ave.
Oklahoma City, OK 73132
405-728-4895
1-800-654-8268
Fax: 405-728-4878

**Rocktile Specialty
Products**
220 S. Ave. A
Boise, ID 83702

**Rockwood Retaining
Walls**
7200 N. Hwy. 63
Rochester, MN 55906
507-288-8850
1-800-535-2375
Fax: 507-288-3810
www.retainingwall.com

Rod McLellan Co.
914 S. Claremont Ave.
San Mateo, CA 94402
650-373-3900
1-877-864-1694

Fax: 415-543-6836
www.rodmclellan.com

RoLanka Intl.
365 Toccoa Pl.
Jonesboro, GA 30236
770-506-8211
1-800-760-3215
Fax: 770-506-0391
www.rolanka.com

Ros-Equus
40350 Wilderness Rd.
Branscomb, CA 95417

**Roses of Yesterday &
Today**
803 Brown's Valley Rd.
Watsonville, CA 95076
831-728-1901
www.rosesofyesterday.
com

Roses Unlimited
Rt. 1, Box 587
Laurens, SC 29360
864-682-7673
Fax: 864-682-2455
www.members.aol.com/
rosesunlmt/index.htm

Rota-Trim Sales
P.O. Box 16365
Lubbock, TX 79490-6365
806-762-3698
Fax: 806-762-0775

Rotocast
Terracast
4700 Mitchell St.
North Las Vegas, NV
89030
702-643-2644
1-800-423-8539
Fax: 702-643-2641
www.rotocast.com/
teracast

Roy Electric Co.
1054 Coney Island Ave.
Brooklyn, NY 11230
718-434-7002
1-800-366-3347
Fax: 718-421-4678

Royal Crown Limited
Triple Crown®
Fence/Brock Decke
Systems
P.O. Box 360
Milford, IN 46542-0360
219-658-9442
1-800-365-3625
Fax: 877-725-3325
www.royalcrownltd.com

**Royalston Oak Timber
Frames**
N. Fitzwilliam Rd.
Royalston, MA
01331-9527
508-249-9633
Fax: 508-249-9633

R. Seawright Gardens
P.O. Box 733
201 Bedford Rd.
Carlisle, MA 01741-0733
978-369-1900
Fax: 978-369-0915
E-mail:
seawrightr@aol.com

Ryan Forest Products
(A Div. of Kenora Forest
Products)
165 Ryan St.
Winnipeg, MB R2R 0N9
Canada
204-989-9600
1-800-665-0273
Fax: 204-694-7232

**S. Parker Hardware
Mfg. Corp.**
PO Box 9882, Parker Dr.
Englewood, NJ 07631
201-569-1600
Fax: 201-569-1082
E-mail:sparker@crusoe.net

S & S Seeds
P.O. Box 1275
Carpinteria, CA
93014-1275
805-684-0436
Fax: 805-684-2798
www.ss-seeds.com

Salt Spring Seeds
Box 444, Ganges
Salt Spring Island, BC
V8K 2W1 Canada
250-537-5269

Samax Enterprises
62 Woolsey St.
Irvington, NJ 07111
973-371-8999
1-800-545-7658
Fax: 973-399-5872
www.rockmiracle.com

**Sandy Mush Herb
Nursery**
316 Surrett Cove Rd.
Leicester, NC 28748-5517
828-683-2014

Sansher Corp.
8005 N. Clinton St.
Fort Wayne, IN 46825
219-484-2000
Fax: 219-482-6780

Santa Barbara Greenhouses
721 Richmond Ave.
Oxnard, CA 93030
805-483-4288
1-800-544-5276

Sarnafil
100 Dan Rd.
Canton, MA 02021
781-828-5400
1-800-451-2504
Fax: 781-828-5365
www.sarnafilus.com

Saxton Gardens
1 First St.
Saratogo Springs, NY 12866
518-584-4697

Scag Power Equipment
1000 Metalcraft Dr.
Mayville, WI 53050-2354
920-387-0100
Fax: 920-387-0111
www.scagpowerequipment.com

Scatton Bros. Awning Mfg.
284 Wissahickon Ave.
P.O. Box 1428
North Wales, PA 19454
215-699-9211
1-800-523-2280
Fax: 215-699-9215

Schlabach's Nursery
3901 Country Rd. 135
Millersburg, OH 44654-9217

Schluter Systems
194 Pleasant Ridge Rd.
Plattsburgh, NY 12901-5841
514-695-2100
1-800-361-3127
Fax: 514-630-0983
www.schluter.com

Schreiner's Iris Gardens
3625 Quinaby Rd. N.E.
Salem, OR 97303
503-393-3232
1-800-525-2367
Fax: 503-393-5590

Schweiss Co.
P.O. Box 557
Sherburn, MN 56171-0557
507-764-2251
Fax: 507-764-2252
Only in Midwest

Scott Sign Systems
P.O. Box 1047
Tallevast, FL 34270-1047
941-355-5171
1-800-237-9447
Fax: 941-351-1787
www.scottsigns.com

Sea Born/Lane
1601 13th Ave.
Charles City, IA 50616
515-228-2000
1-800-457-5013
Fax: 515-228-4417
www.salamander.com/~nutz/seaborn.htm

Sea Gull Lighting Products
P.O. Box 329
301 W. Washington St.
Riverside, NJ 08075
609-764-0500
1-800-347-5483
Fax: 800-877-4855
www.seagulllighting.com

Seeds Trust: High Altitude Gardens
P.O. Box 1048
Hailey, ID 83333
208-788-4363
Fax: 208-788-3452
Internet: http://www.seedsave.org

Select Seeds - Antique Flowers
180 Stickney Rd.
Union, CT 06076
Fax: 860-684-9224
www.selectseeds.com

Serra Gardens Cacti & Succulents
By Appointment to the Trade
Malibu, CA 90265
310-456-1572
www.cacti.com

Seton Identification Products
P.O. Box 819
Branford, CT 06405-0819
203-488-8059
1-800-243-6624
Fax: 203-488-5973
Internet: http://www.seton.com

SF Concrete Technology
2155 Dunwin Dr., Ste. 25
Mississauga, ON L5L 4M1
Canada
905-828-2868
1-888-FIRST SF

Fax: 905-828-0696
www.sf-kooperation.de

Shady Oaks Nursery
112 10th Ave. S.E.
Waseca, MN 56093
507-835-5033
1-800-504-8006
Fax: 507-835-8772
www.shadyoaks.com

Sheffield Bronze Paint Corp.
PO Box 19206
17814 S. Waterloo Rd.
Cleveland, OH 44119-0206
216-481-8330
Fax: 216-481-6606

Shein's Cactus
3360 Drew St.
Marina, CA 93933
408-384-7765

Shelter King
(A Div. of Crop King)
5050 Greenwich Rd.
Seville, OH 44273
330-769-2002
Fax: 330-769-2616

Shepard Iris Garden
3342 W. Orangewood
Phoenix, AZ 85051
Zip: 06790-6658
602-841-1231
Fax: 602-841-1231

Shepherd's Garden Seeds
30 Irene St.
Torrington, CT 06790
860-482-3638
Fax: 860-482-0532
www.shepherdseeds.com

The Sherwin-Williams Co.
101 Prospect Ave., N.W.
Cleveland, OH 44115
216-566-2000
1-800-336-1110

Shooting Star Nursery
444 Bates Rd.
Frankfort, KY 40601
502-223-1679

Shredit Rotary Mower Blades
4863 Fulton Dr. N.W.
Canton, OH 44718-2382
330-492-8806
1-800-869-6621
Fax: 330-492-0205
www.image-video.com/shredit

Signs by Mayo
9217 N. Laramie Ave.
Skokie, IL 60077
847-470-1500
Fax: 847-470-1515
E-mail:mayop@starnetinc.com

Silver Springs Nursery
HCR 62, Box 86
Moyie Springs, ID 83845
208-267-5753
Fax: 208-267-5753
E-mail:ssninc@dmi.net

Simplicity Mfg.
Box 997
Port Washington, WI 53074-0997
414-284-8669
Fax: 414-377-8202
www.simplicitymfg.com

Simpson Strong-Tie Co.
4637 Chabot Dr., Ste. 200
Pleasanton, CA 94588-2749
510-460-9912
1-800-999-5099
Fax: 510-847-0694
www.strongtie.com

Sir Williams Gardens
2852 Jackson Blvd.
Highland, MI 48356
248-887-4779

Sitecraft Corp.
40-25 Crescent St.
Long Island City, NY 11101
718-729-4900
1-800-221-1448
Fax: 718-482-0661

SkyQuest
811 E. Waterman
Wichita, KS 67202
316-636-4244
1-800-279-8568
Fax: 316-262-2653

Skytech Systems
7030 New Berwick Hwy.
Bloomsburg, PA 17815-8630
717-752-1111
1-800-447-4938
Fax: 717-752-3535

Slocum Water Gardens
1101 Cypress Gardens Blvd.
Winter Haven, FL 33884
941-293-7151
Fax: 941-299-1896
Fax: 800-322-1896

Slope Block
280 Asta Ave.
Newbury Park, CA 91320
805-376-9924
805-499-0864

Smart Deck Systems
2600 W. Roosevelt Rd.
Chicago, IL 60608
312-491-2500
1-888-7DECKING
Fax: 312-491-2501
www.smartdeck.com

SNOC
17200 Centrale
St-Hyacinthe, PQ J2T 4J7
Canada
514-774-5238
Fax: 514-774-1954

Snorkel Stove Co.
4216 Sixth Ave. S.
Seattle, WA 98108-1701
206-340-0981
1-800-962-6208
Fax: 206-340-0982
www.snorkel.com

Soils Plus Recycling
P.O. Box 432
Fulton, CA 95439-0432
707-525-8330
Fax: 707-525-0838

**Solar Energy
Industries Assn.**
122 C St., N.W., Fourth Fl.
Washington, DC 20001
202-383-2600
Fax: 202-383-2670
www.seia.org

Solarcone
P.O. Box 67
Seward, IL 61077-0067
815-247-8454
1-800-807-6527
Fax: 815-247-8443

Sonneborn/ChemRex
889 Valley Park Dr.
Shakopee, MN 55379
612-496-6000
1-800-433-9517
Fax: 800-496-6067

Sonoma Grapevines
P.O. Box 293
Fulton, CA 95439-0293
707-542-5510
Fax: 707-542-4801
www.
sonomagrapevines.com

Soules Garden
5809 Rahke Rd.
Indianapolis, IN 46217

317-786-7839

Southeast Wood
3077 Carter Hill Rd.
Montgomery, AL 36111
334-269-9663
1-800-444-0409
Fax: 334-832-9703
Only in Midwest, South, East

Southern Barks
P.O. Box 724
Wiggins, MS 39577-0724
601-928-7171
Only in South

Southern Intl.
1252 Ave. T
Grand Prairie, TX 75050
972-641-2611
1-800-888-0387
Fax: 972-641-3869

Southern Pine Council
PO Box 641700
Kenner, LA 70064-1700
504-443-4464
Fax: 504-443-6612
www.southernpine.com

**Southern Sales &
Marketing Group**
4400 Commerce Cir. S.W.
Atlanta, GA 30336
404-505-5900
Fax: 404-505-5925

Southland Mower
P.O. Box 347
Selma, AL 36702-0347
334-874-7405
Fax: 334-874-7409
www.vulcaninc.com

**Southland Spa &
Sauna**
P.O. Box 638
Ray Farm Rd.
Haleyville, AL 35565
205-486-7919
Fax: 205-486-7795

SouthWood Corp.
P.O. Box 410888
Charlotte, NC 28241-0888
704-588-5000
1-800-727-6884
Fax: 704-588-5017

Sovebec
9201 Boul. Du Centre
Hospitalier
Charny, PQ G6X 1L5
Canada
418-832-6181
Fax: 418-832-1456
www.sovebec.com

**Spiral Stairs of
America**
1700 Spiral Ct.
Erie, PA 16510
814-898-3700
1-800-722-3700
Fax: 814-899-9139
www.spiralstairsofamerica.
com

Spruce Gardens
2317 3rd Rd.
Wisner, NE 68791-3536
402-529-6860

St. Thomas Creations
1022 W. 24th St., Ste. 125
National City, CA
91950-6302
619-474-9490
1-800-536-2284
Fax: 619-474-9493

Stanco Inc.
2738 19th St. S.E.
Salem, OR 97302-1504
503-378-1602
1-800-443-7826
Fax: 503-399-8931
www.stanco-inc.com

**Standard Tar
Products Co.**
2456 W. Cornell St.
Milwaukee, WI
53209-6294
414-873-7650
1-800-825-7650
Fax: 414-873-7737

Starfire Lighting
317 St. Pauls Ave.
Jersey City, NJ 07306
1-800-443-8823
Fax: 201-656-0666

**Steel & Wire
Products Co.**
P.O. Box 207
1501 W. Patapsco Ave.
Baltimore, MD 21203
410-355-2800
Fax: 410-355-1880

**Steiner Turf
Equipment**
289 N. Kurzen Rd.
P.O. Box 504
Dalton, OH 44618-0504
330-828-0200
Fax: 330-828-1008
www.steinerturf.com

**Steptoe & Wife
Antiques**
322 Geary Ave.
Toronto, ON M6H 2C7
Canada

416-530-4200
1-800-461-0060
Fax: 416-530-4666
www.steptoewife.com

STO Finish Systems
(A Div. of STO Corp.)
6175 Riverside Dr. S.W.
Atlanta, GA 30331
404-346-3666
1-800-221-2397
Fax: 404-346-3119

Stock Seed Farms
28008 Mill Rd.
Murdock, NE 68407
402-867-3771
Fax: 402-867-2442
www.stockseed.com

**Stone Construction
Equipment**
32 E. Main St.
P.O. Box 150
Honeoye, NY 14471
716-229-5141
1-800-888-9926
Fax: 716-229-2363
www.stone-equip.com

Stone Forest
Dept. K, P.O. Box 2840
Santa Fe, NM 87504
505-986-8883
Fax: 505-982-2712
www.stoneforest.com

Stonewear, Inc.
2900 Lockheed Way
Carson City, NV 89706
702-883-8300
1-800-356-2462
Fax: 702-883-8306
www.stonewear.com

**Straubel Stone
Lightweight**
1500 E. Chestnut Ave.
No. A
Santa Ana, CA
92701-6321
714-550-6790
1-800-640-POTS
Fax: 714-550-6794
www.straubelstone.com

Streator Unlimited
P.O. Box 706
Streator, IL 61364-0706
815-673-5574
Fax: 815-673-1714
Only in Midwest

**Strom Plumbing By
Sign Of The Crab**
Dept. RM, 3756 Omec Cir.
Rancho Cordova, CA
95742-7399

916-638-2722
1-800-843-2722
Fax: 916-638-2725
www.signofthecrab.com

Style-Mark
960 W. Barre
Archbold, OH 43502
419-445-0116
1-800-446-3040
Fax: 419-445-4440

Summitville Tiles
P.O. Box 73
Summitville, OH 43962
330-223-1511
Fax: 330-223-1414
www.summitville.com

Sun Garden Specialities
P.O. Box 52382
Tulsa, OK 74152
1-800-468-1638

Sun Room Co.
P.O. Box 301
Leola, PA 17540
717-391-7035
1-800-426-2737
Fax: 717-391-7039

Sun Room Designs
Depot & First Sts.
Youngwood, PA 15697
412-925-1100
1-800-621-1110
Fax: 412-925-9172
www.sunroomdesigns.com

Sunbilt Solar Products by Sussman
109-10 180th St.
Jamaica, NY 11433
718-297-6040
Fax: 718-297-3090

Sundance Supply
HC1, Box 116
Olga, WA 98279
1-800-776-2534
Fax: 800-775-4479
www.sundancesupply.com

Sunesta Products
11320 Distribution Ave. E.
Jacksonville, FL 32256
904-268-8000
1-800-874-2001
Fax: 904-260-4499

Sunrise Nursery
13105 Canyon View
Leander, TX 78641
512-267-0023
www.flash.net/~snrsnrsy

Sunset Moulding Co.
P.O. Box 327
Live Oak, CA 95953
530-695-1000
1-800-824-5888
Fax: 530-695-2560

Sunshine Farm & Gardens
RT 5HP
Renick, WV 24966
304-497-2208
Fax: 304-497-2698
www.gardenweb.com/sunshine/

Sunshine Garden House
P.O. Box 2068
Longview, WA 98632
1-888-272-9333
Fax: 360-577-4244
www.gardenhouse.com

Sunshine Rooms
3333 N. Mead
Wichita, KS 67219
316-838-0033
1-800-222-1598
Fax: 316-838-0839

Sunstar Lighting
1723A N.W. 33rd St.
Pompano Beach, FL 33064
954-972-6136
1-800-881-7827
Fax: 954-968-8321

SunTuf
30 W. Mt. Pleasant Ave.
Ste. 201
Livingston, NJ 07039
201-535-8222
1-800-278-6883
Fax: 201-535-6124

Superior Aluminum Products
555 E. Main St.
P.O. Box 430
Russia, OH 45363
937-526-4065
Fax: 937-526-3904
www.wesnet.com/superioraluminum/

Superior Concrete Products
P.O. Box 201625
Arlington, TX 76006
817-277-9255
Fax: 817-261-0194
www.concretefence.com

Superior Controls Co.
24950 Ave. Kearney
Valencia, CA 91355

Super-Tek Products
25-44 Borough Pl.
Woodside, NY 11377-7899
718-278-7900
Fax: 718-204-6013

Superthrive
5411 Satsuma Ave.
North Hollywood, CA 91603
213-877-5186
1-800-441-8482
Fax: 818-766-8482
www.vitamininstitute.com

Supreme Decking
P.O. Box 1459
Lorton, VA 22079
1-800-532-1323
Fax: 703-339-5712

Surebond
500 E. Remington Rd.
Schaumburg, IL 60173
708-843-1818
Fax: 708-843-0765

Sure-Lites
(A Div. of Cooper Lighting)
400 Busse Rd.
Elk Grove Village, IL 60007
708-956-8400
Fax: 708-956-1537

Sure-Loc Edging Corp.
A5482 144th Ave.
Holland, MI 49423
800-787-3562
1-800-787-3562
Fax: 616-392-6015
www.surelocedging.com

Swanns' Daylily Garden
P.O. Box 7686
Warner Robins, GA 31095-7686
912-953-4778
www.gardeneureka.com

Sweepster
2800 Zeeb Rd.
Dexter, MI 48130-9797
734-996-9116
1-800-456-7100
Fax: 734-996-9014
E-mail:sweep@sweepster.com

SwimEx Systems
Rt. 136 Market St.
P.O. Box 328
Warren, RI 02885
401-245-7946
1-800-877-7946
Fax: 401-245-3160

Swivelier
P.O. Box 619
Nanuet, NY 10954-0619
914-623-3471
Fax: 914-623-1861
E-mail:swivelier@juno.com

Sylvan Designs
8921 Quartz Ave.
Northridge, CA 91324
818-998-6868
Fax: 818-998-7241

Systematic Irrigation Controls
P.O. Box 8051
Newport Beach, CA 92660
714-347-1922
Fax: 714-347-1941

Targetti USA
1513 East St. Gertrude Place
Santa Ana, CA 92705
1-800-854-3288
Fax: 714-754-0258

Tarheel Wood Treating Co.
10309 Chapel Hill Rd.
P.O. Box 480
Morrisville, NC 27560
919-467-9176
Fax: 919-467-6707
Only in South

Task Lighting Corp.
P.O. Box 1090
Kearney, NE 68848
308-236-6707
1-800-445-6404
Fax: 308-234-9401
www.tasklighting.com

Texas Greenhouse Co.
2524 White Settlement Rd.
Ft. Worth, TX 76107
817-335-5447
1-800-227-5447
Fax: 817-334-0818
www.texasgreenhouse.com

Textron Turf Corp. and Specialty Products
1721 Packard Ave.
Racine, WI 53403-2564
1-888-922-TURF

Thermal Industries
301 Brushton Ave.
Pittsburgh, PA 15221
412-244-6400
1-800-245-1540
Fax: 412-244-6496
Only in Midwest, South, East

Thermal-Gard
400 Walnut St.
Punxsutawney, PA
15767-1368
814-938-1408
Fax: 814-938-1428

Thomas Lighting
Consumer Div.
950 Breckinridge Ln.
Ste. G50
Louisville, KY 40207
502-894-2400
1-800-36LIGHT
Fax: 502-894-2427
www.thomaslighting.com

Thompson and Morgan Inc.
P.O. Box 1308
Jackson, NJ 08527
1-800-274-7333
Fax: 732-363-9356

Thundering Springs Daylily Garden
1056 South Lake Dr.
Dublin, GA 31027-2509
912-272-1526
E-mail:ebrown@planttel.net

Tilley's Nursery/The Waterworks
111 E. Fairmount St.
Coopersburg, PA 18036
610-282-4784
Fax: 610-282-1262
Only in East

Timber Press
133 S.W. Second Ave.
Suite 450
Portland, OR 97204
503-227-2878
1-800-327-5680
Fax: 503-227-3070
www.timberpress.com

Timberhouse Post & Beam
150 Sheafman Creek Rd.
Victor, MT 59875
406-961-3276
Fax: 406-961-4643

TIR Systems
3350 Bridgeway St.
Vancouver, BC V5K 1H9
Canada
604-294-8477
1-800-663-2036
Fax: 604-294-3733

Tivoli Industries
1513 East St. Gertrude Pl.
Santa Ana, CA 92705
800-854-3288

Fax: 714-754-0258

Todd Valley Farms
P.O. Box 202, E. Hwy. 92
Mead, NE 68041-0202
402-624-6385
Fax: 402-624-2003
www.toddvalleyfarms.com

Tollmark Corp.
P.O. Box 2295
Prescott, AZ 86302
520-445-7323
1-800-477-7723
Fax: 520-778-9477

Topiaries Unlimited
RD 2, Box 40C
Pownal, VT 05261
802-823-5536
Fax: 802-823-5080
E-mail:kwheld@sover.net

TR Miller Mill Co.
P.O. Box 708
Brewton, AL 36427
205-867-1227
Fax: 205-867-6882

Tree Pro
3180 W. 250 North
West Lafayette, IN 47906
765-463-1011
1-800-875-8071
Fax: 765-463-3157

Treessentials Co.
2371 Waters Dr.
Mendota Heights, MN
55120-1163
651-681-0011
1-800-248-8239
Fax: 651-681-1951
www.treessentials.com

Trenwyth Industries
1 Connelly Rd.
P.O. Box 438
Emigsville, PA 17318
717-767-6868
1-800-233-1924
Fax: 717-767-4023

Trex Co.
20 S. Cameron
Winchester, VA 22601
540-678-4070
1-800-BUY-TREX
Fax: 540-678-1820
www.trex.com

Trimblehouse Corp.
4658 S. Old Peachtree Rd.
Norcross, GA 30071
770-448-1972
1-800-241-4317
Fax: 770-447-9250

Triple Crown Fence
Royal Crown Ltd.
P.O. Box 360
State Rd. 15 N.
Milford, IN 46542-0360
219-658-9442
1-800-365-3625
Fax: 219-658-3147
www.royalcrownltd.com

Tru-Cut
P.O. Box 65647
Los Angeles, CA
90065-0647
323-258-4135
Fax: 323-258-3376

Trus Joist MacMillan
P.O. Box 60
Boise, ID 83706
208-364-1200
1-800-338-0515
Fax: 208-364-1300
www.tjm.com

Tubco Whirlpools
2870 Slough St.
Mississauga, ON L4T 1G3
Canada
905-677-3333
Fax: 905-677-4852
E-mail:massoud@netcom.com

Turner Greenhouses
P.O. Box 1260
Goldsboro, NC 27533
919-734-8345
1-800-672-4770
Fax: 919-736-4550
www.turnergreenhouses.com

Unicel
88 Rue de Vaudreuil
Boucherville, PQ J4B 5G4
Canada
514-655-1580
1-800-668-1580
Fax: 514-655-0162

Uni-Group USA
4362 Northlake Blvd.
No. 207
Palm Beach Gardens, FL
33410
561-626-4666
1-800-USA-1UNI
Fax: 561-627-6403
E-mail:unigroup@siservices.net

UNITEC
Bahia de Todos Los Santos
No. 26
Col. V. Anzures, Mexico
City, DF 11300 Mexico
011.52.5.545-1009

Fax: 011.5 2.5.531-9622

United Gilsonite Laboratories
P.O. Box 70
Scranton, PA 18501-0070
717-344-1202
1-800-845-5227
Fax: 717-969-7634
www.ugl.com

Universal Forest Products
2801 E. Beltline, N.E.
Grand Rapids, MI
49525-9736
616-364-6161
1-800-598-9663
Fax: 616-361-8302

Upper Hand Marketing
7620 University Ave. N.E.
Fridley, MN 55432-2655
612-571-7637
1-800-685-0315
Fax: 612-571-5477
www.rakehandle.com

The Urban Homestead
818 Cumberland St.
Bristol, VA 24201
540-466-2931
Only in South, East

U.S. Gaslight
4658 S. Old Peachtree Rd.
Norcross, GA 30071
770-448-1972
1-800-241-4317
Fax: 770-447-9250

US Sky
(A Div. of Stora
Enterprises Co.)
2907 Agua Fria
Santa Fe, NM 87501
505-471-5711
1-800-323-5017
Fax: 505-471-5437

Valley View Industries
13834 S. Kostner Ave.
Crestwood, IL 60445-1997
708-597-0885
1-800-323-9369
Fax: 800-323-3262
www.valleyviewind.com

Van Bourgondien Bros.
Box 1000
Babylon, NY 11702
1-800-622-9997
Fax: 516-669-1228
www.dutchbulbs.com

Van Dyke Zinnias
@ Redbud Farms
3820 Stillson Rd.
Stockbridge, MI 49285
517-851-8194
E-mail:sballer@lobatek.
com

**Van Ness Water
Gardens**
2460 N. Euclid Ave.
Upland, CA 91784
909-982-2425
1-800-205-2425
Fax: 909-949-7217
www.vnwg.com

Van Well Nursery
P.O. Box 1339
Wenatchee, WA
98807-1339
509-886-8189
1-800-572-1553
Fax: 509-886-0294
www.vanwell.net

Vandermolen Corp.
119 Dorsa Ave.
Livingston, NJ
07039-1002
973-992-4219
Fax: 973-992-4219

Vegetable Factory
495 Post Rd. E.
Westport, CT 06880-4400
203-454-0040
1-800-221-2550
Fax: 203-454-0020

**Vernon Barnes and
Son Nursery**
P.O. Box 250S6
McMinnville, TN 37110
931-668-8576
Fax: 931-668-2165

Versadek Industries
P.O. Box 730743
San Jose, CA 95173-0743
1-800-497-3325
Fax: 800-977-1960

**Versa-Lok Retaining
Wall Systems**
6348 Hwy. 36, Suite 1
Oakdale, MN 55128
612-770-3166
1-800-770-4525
Fax: 612-770-4089
versa-lok.com

Vesey's Seeds
P.O. Box 9000
Calais, ME 04619
902-368-7333
1-800-363-7333
Fax: 902-566-1620
www.veseys.com

**Vileniki—An Herb
Farm**
Rd. 1, Box 354
Montdale, PA 18447
717-254-9895
Fax: 717-254-9895
E-mail:
vilhrbfarm@aol.com

Villagecraft Industries
P.O. Box 707
State College, PA 16804
814-353-1777
1-800-458-9396
Fax: 814-692-4414

VinylGard
1576 Magnolia Dr.
Macon, MS 39341
1-800-563-3623
Fax: 601-726-9856
E-mail:
odtech@ebicom.net

Vinyl Tech/PGT
P.O. Box 1529
Nokomis, FL 34274
941-493-4858
Fax: 941-497-3655

The Violet House
P.O. Box 1274
Gainesville, FL 32602
352-377-8465
1-800-377-8466
Fax: 352-372-0102
E-mail:violethous@aol.
com

Vixen Hill Gazebos
Dept CG-7, Main Street
Elverson, PA 19520
610-286-0909
1-800-423-2766
Fax: 610-282-2099
www.vixenhill.com

WAC Lighting Co.
P.O. Box 560218
113-25 14th Ave.
College Point, NY 11356
718-961-0695
1-800-526-2588
Fax: 800-526-2585
E-mail:waclgt@aol.com

**Wagoner Floor Safety
Systems**
P.O. Box 2784
Reno, NV 89505
702-878-4768

Waldo & Assoc
28214 Glenwood Rd.
Perrysburg, OH
43551-4855
419-666-3662

Walker Mfg. Co.
5925 E. Harmony Rd.
Ft. Collins, CO
80528-9569
970-221-5614
1-800-279-8537
Fax: 970-221-5619
www.walkermowers.com

Wall Firma
733 E. Main St.
Monongahela, PA 15063
412-258-6873
1-800-333-4333
Fax: 412-258-3188
Only in Midwest, South, East

Waterfall Creations
P.O. Box 32
Occoquan, VA
22125-0032
703-718-0209

Watertech
2507 Plymouth Rd.
Johnson City, TN 37601
1-800-BUY-TUBS
Fax: 615-926-1470

Wausau Tile
P.O. Box 1520
Wausau, WI 54402-1520
715-359-3121
1-800-388-8728
Fax: 715-355-4627

Wavecrest Nursery
2509 Lakeshore Dr.
Fennville, MI 49408
616-543-4175
Fax: 616-543-4100

Weatherall Co.
6820 S. Jasmine Ct.
Englewood, CO 80112
1-800-399-8609
Fax: 303-740-6019

Weathermatic Co.
P.O. Box 180205
Dallas, TX 75218
214-278-6131
Fax: 214-271-5710

We-Du Nursery
Rt. 5, Box 724
Marion, NC 28752
Fax: 828-738-8131
www.we-du.com

**Wellington Leisure
Products**
P.O. Box 244
Madison, GA 30650-0244
706-342-1916
Fax: 706-342-4047
www.wellingtoninc.com

**Western Red Cedar
Lumber Assn.**
1100-555 Burrard St.
Vancouver, BC V7X 1S7
Canada
604-684-0266
Fax: 604-682-8641
www.cofi.org/wrcla

**Western Wood
Products Assn.**
522 S.W. Fifth Ave.
Ste. 400
Portland, OR 97204
503-224-3930
Fax: 503-224-3934

Westview Products
P.O. Box 569
Dallas, OR 97338
503-623-5174
1-800-203-7557
Fax: 503-623-3382

Wheeler Arts
66 Lake Park
Champaign, IL
61822-7132
217-359-6816
Fax: 217-359-8716
www.users.aol.com/
quickart

Whitacre-Greer
1400 S. Mahoning Ave.
Alliance, OH 44601

White Flower Farm
P.O. Box 50
Litchfield, CT 06759
860-496-9624
1-800-503-9624
Fax: 860-496-1418
www.whiteflowerfarm.
com

White Oak Nursery
6145 W. Oak Point Rd.
Peoria, IL 61614-3531
309-693-1354
Fax: 309-693-0993
E-mail:
whiteoak5@aol.com

**Wicklein's Water
Gardens**
P.O. Box 9780
Baldwin, MD 21013
410-823-1335
1-800-382-6716
Fax: 410-823-1427
wickleinaquatics.com

Wikco Industries
4930 N. 57th St.
Lincoln, NE 69507-3101
402-464-2070
Fax: 402-464-2070
www.wikco.com

Wildflower Nursery
1680 Hwy. 25-70
Marshall, NC 28753
828-656-2723
Fax: 828-656-2723

**The Wildflower
Seed Co.**
P.O. Box 406
St. Helena, CA 94574
707-963-3359
1-800-456-3359
Fax: 707-963-5383
www.wildflower-seed.com

Wildseed Farms
425 Wildflower Hills
P.O. Box 3000
Fredericksburg, TX
78624-3000
830-990-8080
1-800-848-0078
Fax: 830-990-8090
www.wildseedfarms.com

Wildwood Gardens
P.O. Box 250
Molalla, OR 97038-0250
503-829-3102
E-mail:gardens@molalla.
net

Willhite Seed
P.O. Box 23
Poolville, TX 76487-0023
817-599-8656
1-800-828-1840
Fax: 817-599-5843
www.willhiteseed.com

William Dam Seeds
P.O. Box 8400
Dundas, ON L9H 6M1
Canada
905-628-6641
Fax: 905-627-1729
E-mail:willdam@
sympatico.ca

William Zinsser & Co.
173 Belmont Dr.
Somerset, NJ 08875
732-469-4367
Fax: 732-563-9774
www.zinsser.com

**Willow Oak Flower &
Herb Farm**
8109 Telegraph Rd.
Severn, MD 21144
410-551-2237

Wind and Weather
P.O. Box 2320
Mendocino, CA 95460
1-800-922-9463
Fax: 707-964-1278
www.windandweather.com

Windleaves
7560 Morningside Dr.
Indianapolis, IN 46240
317-251-1381

Windrose
1093 Mill Rd.
Pen Argyl, PA 18072
610-588-1037
Fax: 610-599-0968
E-mail:windrose@epix.net

Windy Oaks Aquatics
W. 377 S-10677 Betts Rd.
Eagle, WI 53119
414-594-3033
Fax: 414-594-3414

Winged Weeder
1577 W. Sunnyside Rd.
Idaho Falls, ID
83402-4349
208-523-0526
1-800-388-4539
Fax: 208-522-5096
www.wingedweeder.com

**Winn Soldani's Fancy
Hibiscus**
1142 S.W. 1st Ave.
Pompano Beach, FL
  33060
954-782-0741
Fax: 954-782-7639
www.fancyhibiscus.com

**Wolman Wood Care
Products**
436 Seventh Ave.
No. 1824
Pittsburgh, PA
15219-1818
412-227-2427
Fax: 412-227-2618

Womanswork
P.O. Box 543
York, ME 03909

**Wood Innovations of
Suffolk**
P.O. Box 356
Medford, NY 11763
516-698-2345
Fax: 516-698-2396
www.woodin.com

Wood Prairie Farm
RFD 7, Box 164
Bridgewater, ME 04735
207-429-9765
1-800-829-9765
Fax: 800-300-6494
www.woodprairie.com

Wood Violet Books
3814 Sunhill Dr.
Madison, WI 53718
608-837-7207
E-mail:wvbooks@aol.com

Woodcraft Supply
210 Wood County
  Industrial Park
P.O. Box 1686
Parkersburg, WV 26102
304-428-4866
1-800-225-1153
Fax: 304-428-8271

Wood-Kote Products
8000 N.E. 14th Pl.
Portland, OR 97211
503-285-8371
Fax: 503-285-8374
www.woodkote.com

Woodlanders
1128 Colleton Ave.
Aiken, SC 29801
803-648-7522
Fax: 803-648-7522

Worthington Group
P.O. Box 868
Troy, AL 36081
334-566-4537
1-800-872-1608
Fax: 334-566-5390
www.
architectural-details.com

WR Bonsal Co.
8201 Arrowridge Blvd.
P.O. Box 241148
Charlotte, NC 28224-1148
704-525-1621
1-800-738-1621
Fax: 704-529-5261
Only in South

WR Meadows, Inc.
P.O. Box 543
Elgin, IL 60121
847-683-4500
1-800-342-5976
Fax: 847-683-4544

Xypex Chemical Corp.
13731 Mayfield Pl.
Richmond, BC V6V 2G9
Canada
604-273-5265
1-800-961-4477
Fax: 604-270-0451
www.xypex.com

Yenkin Majestic
1920 Leonard Ave.
Columbus, OH 43219
614-253-8511
Fax: 614-253-6327

Yeoman & Co.
P.O. Box 30
Monticello, IA
52310-0030
319-465-3553
1-800-367-9646
Fax: 319-465-5284
www.yo-ho.com

Zynolyte Paints
2320 E. Dominquez St.
Carson, CA 90810
310-513-0700
1-888-996-6598
Fax: 310-513-1593
www.zynolyte.com

Book & Software Index

BOOKS

agAccess Book Catalog
P.O. Box 2008
Davis, CA 95617
530-756-7177
1-800-540-0170
Fax: 530-756-7188
www.agribooks.com

The American Botanist, Booksellers
P.O. Box 532
1103 W. Truitt Ave.
Chillicothe, IL 61523
309-274-5254
Fax: 309-274-6143
E-mail:agbook@mtco.com

Brent and Becky's Bulbs
7463 Heath Trail
Gloucester, VA 23061
804-693-3966
Fax: 804-693-9436
E-mail:bbheath@aol.com

Brooks Books
P.O. Box 91
Clayton, CA 94517-0091
925-672-4566
Fax: 925-672-3338
E-mail:brooksbk@netvista.net

Builders Booksource
1817 Fourth St.
Berkeley, CA 94710
510-845-6874
1-800-843-2028
Fax: 510-845-7051
www.buildersbooksite.com

D.V. Burrell Seed Growers Co.
P.O. Box 150-LGG
Rocky Ford, CO 81067
719-254-3318
Fax: 719-254-3319

Elisabeth Woodburn, Books, ABAA
P.O. Box 398
Hopewell, NJ 08525
609-466-0522
E-mail:qege21a@prodigy.com

Elixir Farm Botanicals
General Delivery
Brixey, MO 65618
417-261-2393
1-877-315-SEED
Fax: 417-261-2355
www.elixirfarm.com

Heirloom Seeds
P.O. Box 245
West Elizabeth, PA 15088
412-384-0852
Fax: 412-384-0852
www.heirloomseeds.com

Larry W. Price Books
353 N.W. Maywood Dr.
Portland, OR 97210
503-221-1410
E-mail:lwprice@gateway.net

Linden House Gardening Books
148 Sylvan Ave.
Scarborough, ON
M1M 1K4 Canada
416-269-0699
Fax: 416-269-0615
www.icangarden.com/linden.htm

Raymond M. Sutton, Jr. Books
430 Main St.
Williamsburg, KY
40769-0330
606-549-3464
Fax: 606-549-3469
www.suttonbooks.com

Timber Press
133 S.W. Second Ave.
Suite 450
Portland, OR 97204
503-227-2878
1-800-327-5680
Fax: 503-227-3070
www.timberpress.com

Waterfall Creations
P.O. Box 32
Occoquan, VA
22125-0032
703-718-0209

Wavecrest Nursery
2509 Lakeshore Dr.
Fennville, MI 49408
616-543-4175
Fax: 616-543-4100

Wood Violet Books
3814 Sunhill Dr.
Madison, WI 53718
608-837-7207
E-mail:wvbooks@aol.com

SOFTWARE

Wheeler Arts
66 Lake Park
Champaign, IL
61822-7132
217-359-6816
Fax: 217-359-8716
www.users.aol.com/quickart

Wood Violet Books
3814 Sunhill Dr.
Madison, WI 53718
608-837-7207
E-mail:wvbooks@aol.com

Photo by Maureen Gilmer

Product Index